D1252694

# As Happy

## As You Want To Be!

Marion Sue Jones, MSW
and
John DeFoore, Th.M.

# As Happy

## As You Want To Be!

Marion Sue Jones and John DeFoore, Th.M.
As Happy As You Want To Be!
Copyright © 2002 by Marion Sue Jones and John
DeFoore

All rights reserved.

ISBN 0-9726713-0-7

Title: As Happy As You Want To Be!
Author: Marion Sue Jones and John DeFoore
Subject: Mental health, self-help.

# Dedication

**From John**

My deepest gratitude goes to Telle, my wife and companion of 56 years (who read and reread the book.) Also to my four sons and their families who, at times, have learned from me and other times have taught me — John Jr., Bill and Cindy, Rick and Janet, Shane, Rena, David, Marney and Pam, Ali, Jeni and Becki. You have all loved and cared for me. For that I am most grateful.

**From Marion Sue**

My mother and father gave me a rich heritage of sound principles and values for life that have sustained me in my personal journey, and I am grateful to them for it. I also thank my sons and their families Clayton and Danita, Lindsey, Vivian, Claire; and Clifton and Leah. Their love has always been an anchor for me.

**From Both of Us**

Our lives have been deeply touched and richly blessed by many people who have crossed our paths. Corky Sledge was an invaluable friend who steadfastly loved us and supported us and our work all his life. There were many others who, for more than three decades, have honored us with their friendship. Unfortunately, space will not allow us to list all their names. But there are a few without whom a great deal of what is in this book would not be possible, and so we say a special thank you to Mike and Debbie Rose, Ron and Wynoka Terry, Kreis and Sandy Beall, Merle and Miriam Hinrichs, and Dale Ericson. Bob and Mary Goulding, Dr. Karl Menninger and Dr. Wayne Oates have been great teachers for us. In addition, our hearts have been tied to our "San Angelo, TX Group" with whom we have met for thirty years. We have explored the universe of human thought and feelings with Dale and Kay Bates, Bob and CyBee Hamblen, Joy and Bill Morehead, and Glenn and Carrie Henderson. Our personal journey with them continues, and to them we say thank you. We also acknowledge Deanna Sanford and Vivian Burns who patiently and lovingly have "run" our lives and offices through the years to allow us to do our work. And finally we acknowledge Kay Strom who helped us put this book together. She was patient, kind, helpful and skilled beyond anything we could have expected. Thank you, Kay.

# Table of Contents

# Table of Contents

# 1
# THE PROCESS OF LIFE

*"Happiness is not a feeling, it's a decision."*

"I am so depressed..."

These were Sam's opening words. He quickly continued, "I don't know why. I have no reason to be depressed. I mean, I have a beautiful home, three wonderful children, and a loving wife. I own my own business and financially I'm successful beyond my wildest dreams. Yet inside I feel hollow, empty, and all alone. I'm ashamed to admit it, but it's the truth, and I just had to tell someone."

Sam was living the American dream. He had everything life had to offer—everything, that is, except the main thing. He didn't have

...inner peace
...calmness
...a sense of well-being

Sam didn't have

...happiness.

•

Unfortunately, Sam is not unusual.
Again and again we see people like him
in our office, and we hear them pour out
similar stories.

•

Take Charlotte, for instance.

When we first met Charlotte, her hands shook and her voice trembled as she struggled to speak. "I'm not one for tears," she said as she dabbed impatiently at her eyes. "This isn't at all like me."

Charlotte, a 79-year-old who had lived her entire life on a West Texas ranch, certainly didn't seem the crying type. Browned and weathered by the sun, she drove a truck out every morning at dawn to oversee the running of the ranch just as she had always done. On Saturday nights she played poker, and—until recently—spent Sundays driving the 400-mile round trip to visit her husband in a nursing home.

"Yes, it is hard that my Will died," Charlotte continued. "We were married for 61 years. But he had been awful bad for quite a while now, and I had time to prepare myself. Yet here I am crying all the time. It makes no sense, no sense at all!"

Problems come from different places, and they come in all shapes and sizes. Some, like Charlotte's, are fairly easy to spot. Others, like Sam's, are less so.

Problems can be...

- *external:* "I don't know how long I can deal with a constantly withdrawn spouse."

- *internal:* "I will never get rid of this nagging guilt."

- *personal:* "This is my third marriage, and I don't want it to fail."

- *professional:* "I love my work, but I cannot abide the person who shares my office."

- *irritating:* "My mother telephones me every single day of my life!"

- *catastrophic:* "My son just committed suicide."

- *vague:* "I've got a good job and a great family, but I'm just not happy."

- *specific:* "I work under constant pressure, then I come home and zone out in front of the television with a couple of beers and a bag of potato chips. If I don't make some changes, I'm going to die of a heart attack just like my father did."

Even those of us who are basically satisfied with our lives have areas in which we need to learn. Where are you right now? Do you need to...
- Improve?
- Grow?
- Develop?

•

Then this book is for you.

•

## CHANGE IS POSSIBLE

Charlotte needed to move on with her life. A bright, ambitious woman, she decided to go back to college and finish the degree she had begun half a century before. It meant driving her truck 250 miles roundtrip three times a week, but that didn't daunt her.

Charlotte, at the age of seventy-nine, was making a change.

When we say "change," we're not talking about simply changing a behavior. *We're talking about changing the dynamic that causes the behavior.* Changing a behavior is merely Band-Aid therapy. It covers up the problem, but it does nothing to heal it. Understanding the cause gives you motivation to make changes significant enough to go on to produce the behavioral changes you desire.

This isn't going to happen overnight. It won't even happen in a week. It is a process, a way of life.

•

True change is a journey, a journey that
lasts a lifetime.

•

## STARTING THE JOURNEY

Here is a personal question:

What is it about yourself you want to change? Be specific. Instead of, "I want to be a better person," think, "I want to be more patient and to control my temper."

Make your first commitment by listing three changes you want to see in yourself:

1. _____

   _____

2. _____

   _____

3. _____

## FEELINGS VERSUS ACTIONS

You say you don't feel like you can change? That's not surprising. You are used to the status quo. It feels comfortable to you. This is exactly why so many people remain in destructive or unsatisfying patterns of behavior for their entire lives.

●

You ACT yourself into right feelings,
you don't FEEL your way into right actions.

●

That is why we can so confidently proclaim: ***You are one decision away from happiness.*** Once your brain starts to work toward that goal, you begin to act in ways that will eventually achieve it.

Happiness is a decision you make; it's not a feeling you have.

What exactly is happiness? Here is one definition:

*"Happiness is a deep and abiding sense of inner peace with an overriding feeling of optimism and hope.*

Once the decision is made, the anxiety of questioning your happiness can be set aside and you will be able to enjoy the present.

## BUT IT'S NOT MY FAULT!

*"He* is the reason I'm not happy! If *he* would only change. If *he* would treat me better (would listen to me, would grow up and be responsible), then I would be happy."

It's not *me*, it's...

- my kids
- my emotionally removed husband
- my nagging wife
- my demanding boss
- my critical mother
- my absent father
- my crazy neighbors
- my out-of-control finances
- the crummy place where I live
- my nightmare job
- the spouse who let me down
- the friend I can't trust

Any of these things may be true (hopefully, not all of them!). But *your happiness is not dependent on any of these things*. True, people and circumstances in our lives do affect and influence us, but ultimately each one of us is responsible for our own happiness.

•

No one keeps you from happiness.
You and you alone decide how happy you will be.

•

God did not create us in such a way that our happiness (our feelings) is at the mercy of someone else.

Look over our shoulders and see what we hear in our office:

**Person #1:** *"I would be happy if I were just married.*
**Person #2:** *"I would be happy if I weren't married!*
**Person #3:** *I'd be a lot happier if I didn't have these kids!*
**Person #4:** *"If I only had children, my life would be complete and I'd be happy.*
**Person #5:** *"If I just had that job, I could be happy.*
**Person #6 (with that very job!):** *"I am so unhappy!*

•

Happiness doesn't come from circumstances.
It comes from within.

•

We cannot always control our circumstances. But we
do have control over what we *do* with our circumstances.

## HEALTH, NOT SICKNESS

Picture this:

*Andrew comes into our office and sits down next to
John. He unbuttons the coat of his well-tailored suit, then
nervously adjusts his silk tie.*

*"Tell me about yourself," John says.*

*"I'm a loser," Andrew answers. "Last year I had an affair
with my secretary. My wife found out, and it almost broke
up our marriage. I messed up big time."*

*"I see," says John. "Now tell me, what have you done
that's good?"*

*Andrew looks startled. Then he stammers, "Well, I am the
senior vice-president of the corporation. I have been responsible for adding over 30 new jobs, half of them for people
who were previously considered unemployable."*

*"Wonderful," says John. "What else?"*

*"I have two children. My daughter is in her second year
at a private university and has distinguished herself in engi-
neering. My son is a business major, and this summer he
will be doing an internship at the corporation where I work.
I'm very proud of the people they have become."*

*"That's great," says John. "What else?"*

*"Well, I have been working hard with my wife to repair
our marriage. We both agree it's worth saving."*

Andrew is a humbled man who made a big mistake.
But that is by no means the sum total of who he is. Yet he

sees himself as nothing but a loser.

Over and over people come to our office laboring and struggling under the negative labels stamped on them by others or by themselves. They are allowed to express the negative, then they are told, "That may be true, but tell me about the other part of you."

We don't deny the negative deeds or the illness of an individual, but we don't stop there. We also focus on the person's health and success.

We had the good fortune to study with Dr. Karl Menninger of the Menninger Clinic in Topeka, Kansas. Not only was he a well-respected and wonderfully effective physician, he was also a prolific writer and an all-around wise man. He made a statement with which we totally agree:

•

"More people have been damaged by labels
than have ever been damaged by disease.
And the greatest disservice I can do to a
patient is to give him a label for
his symptoms or problems."

•

Putting labels on people and then sending them out to deal with those labels is an insult to the dignity of the human personality.

Certainly there are people who are unable to function in the everyday world. We recognize that for treatment purposes they may need a diagnosis, and some may need medication. This may be part of the therapeutic process. But most people do not need to be branded with labels that diminish their individual identities.

It can be difficult to throw off a label, especially if it has been in place for a long time. For years a woman we will call Helen had operated under the label of a particular mental disorder. It was true that the mental problem restricted her life, but the label prevented her from pursuing other interests and talents that could have given her a great deal of joy and satisfaction. Again and again Marion Sue urged Helen to tell about the rest of her life. Finally, with her eyes fixed on her tightly clasped hands, Helen whispered that she loved birds, and also the way colors blended and mixed together.

At Marion Sue's encouragement, Helen took watercolor classes. "Now she has a new identity," Marion Sue says.

Yes, the woman still has a mental problem. And, yes, at times it is still a barrier for her. But by strengthening the healthy part of her life rather than focusing on the problem, she has redefined who she is and how she thinks of herself.

Of course, not every problem can be treated this way. We do not ...

- encourage anyone who has been prescribed medication by a physician to stop taking it.

- treat people who are dealing with destructive behavior they cannot control.

- treat people who are abusing alcohol or drugs.

Such people need to be in appropriate treatment programs before they can deal with their underlying dynamics.

What we are saying is that you are a person with many facets. If you dwell solely on your disability, you will be losing the beauty and strength of all those other wonderful sides of yourself.

## JOIN US IN THE PROCESS

We are writing this book out of our training and out of 30 years of experience, and also out of the experiences of the thousands of people with whom we have worked over the years. We, too, are in the process of learning. Like you, we have rejoiced in successes and accomplishments, and we have also faced our share of difficulties, disappointments, and failures.

We invite you to begin the process that can change your life.

# 2
# YOUR LIFE STORY

*"It is vital that your dreams for the future outnumber your memories of the past."*

*Roger was only 18 and just out of high school when he was drafted into the Army. Before his 19th birthday he was fighting for his life in the steaming jungles of Vietnam. For two years he witnessed more horrors than he ever thought possible. The young man who was too squeamish to dissect a frog in biology class was forced to bear witness to horror and slaughter beyond description. When he came home, it was to booing crowds that pelted him with tomatoes.*

*Roger never talked to anyone about his war experiences. "He came through it surprisingly well," people whispered behind his back. Yet whenever a war scene came on television, or even during a fireworks display, he would cower in the closet and cover his head.*

*When Roger's son, Brett, graduated from college, he approached his father and said, "Dad, tell me about the war."*

*"No," said Roger. "I don't want to talk about it."*

*Roger turned to leave, but Brett grabbed his arm. "Please, Dad. I have to know. I have war nightmares all the time."*

*That jarred Roger, for he, too, was plagued with nightmares. So he took his son on a weekend road trip, and he talked and talked and talked. It was the most painful, gut-wrenching thing Roger had ever done. But from that day on, Brett had no more nightmares. Neither did Roger.*

Roger has a unique life story.
So does Brett.
So do you.

That unique story will not stay hidden. Try as we may to hide things from ourselves, they always come out. And when they do, they take back their original form to make themselves evident to ourselves and to others.

•

You are the only you who has ever
been or will ever be.

•

Your life history is yours and yours alone. And good or bad, happy or sad, simple or complex, it is the doorway to your future.

If you really want to make changes in your life, let us show you how to proceed.

## STEP #1: RECORD YOUR LIFE STORY

Write out the events of your entire early life, from your first childhood memories right through until you were grown. Write about the big events and significant people:

- births
- weddings
- illnesses
- deaths
- successes
- failures
- your relationships with your mother and father
- their relationship with each other
- turning points in your life

- the impact other people have had on your life, both positive and negative.
- your sexual history—in detail

But also write about the small ones:

- your first puppy
- the trouble you had in math class
- your friend in fourth grade you trusted with all your secrets only to have him blab them all
- your awkwardness at softball
- honors and awards you received
- your family rituals and routines ("We always....")
- times your family was together as a unit—if there were any

Go back to the earliest time you remember in your childhood. Start there and continue forward until the time you were grown and left home. Include all the events and situations you remember, good, bad and indifferent.

Yes, this is a big assignment, but it's also a very important one. To help get you started, and to guide you along if you get stuck, we have given you a list of ideas, topics, and questions. But don't simply respond to our suggestions. The idea is for you to let your memory run free. Write down anything and everything that comes to mind. Don't worry about whether or not a certain event or memory is important. Just put it down. It's all a part of you, and therefore it *is* important to your life story.

Spend two or three hours on this. Most people end up writing approximately 20 or 25 pages. No one is going to judge or grade this, so don't get hung up on the mechanics of writing. Don't worry about organization, and forget spelling and punctuation rules. Just get your life story down.

The accuracy of your memories makes no difference.

Write the events as you *remember* them. It isn't historical fact that's important; it's how what happened affected you.

•

Your recall shapes your memories,
then your memories dominate your behavior.

•

## QUESTIONS TO CONSIDER:

- Where did you live?

- What was your home like? (It may help to draw an outline of the inside of your house.)

- Where did you play and who did you play with?

- Who were the significant people in your life?

- What specific events were significant and how did they impact you?

- What times of joy and pleasure do you remember?

- What were the traumatic times? The disappointments? The frustrations?

- How old were you when you started school?

- Who took you to school?

- How did you feel about school?

- What were you good at? What did you find difficult?

- Did you ever steal anything when you were a kid? Did you get caught? What happened?

- Write a short character description of your mother. Tell about your relationship with her.

- Write a short character description of your father. Tell about your relationship with him.

- What kind of a relationship did your mother and father have with each other? (Duty-bound? Affectionate? Caretaking? Domineering? Fun? Responsibility-driven?) Write about other significant people in your life (siblings, grandparents, cousins, aunts, uncles, teachers, friends).

- What were you taught about money: Easy come, easy go? That you would never have enough? Be successful and grow rich? Use money frugally? If you've got it, spend it? Manage it well? Give it away? Grasp it tightly and don't let go? Money means success?

- By watching your parents, what did you learn about the value of family? Of friends? About how to treat other people?

- How much inner confidence or security did you have growing up?

- How much ego strength did you get from growing up in your family (by being affirmed, having interest shown in you, being given attention, praised)?

- How did you learn to feel about your body? Was

there an inappropriate emphasis on thinness? Did you decide you were ugly, or that everyone else was attractive and you were not?

• Did you feel like you received the blessing in your family, or were you just an extra? Were you the favorite, the hope of the family who had to live up to everyone's expectations? Was someone else the favored one? Were you the rebel? The black sheep? The smart one? The "slow" one?

• In your family, who touched who physically, and under what circumstances? Was touch limited to punishment? Were you touched as much in tenderness as in punishment?

• Where was the emotionally warm place in your home?

• When you think of your home, where for you was the safest place?

• Who was the warm person in your home (your mother or father, a grandparent, a brother or sister, a maid, the yardman)? Who was the safe one? Who was the fun one?

• What were the crises times in your family (a parent died, a new baby was born, daddy lost his job, the house was sold, parents got a divorce)? Write about losses and changes such as death or divorce, whether in your immediate family or in your extended family.

• Was there order in your home, or was it chaotic?

- Did your parents set boundaries and expect you to keep them in such things as homework, curfews, and bedtimes? Did they guide you towards healthy friendships and away from unhealthy ones?

- Were appropriate "do's" and "don'ts" set down in your home?

- Did your parents make sure the rules were kept?

- What were the consequences for breaking the rules?

- What is your sexual history? (Be as honest and complete as possible.) When and how did you learn the difference between boys and girls? Where did you get your sexual education, and how accurate was it? Did it involve guilt? Did you ever have sexual contact with someone of the same sex? Were there any inappropriate sexual activities, such as being fondled or being taken advantage of sexually?

- Tell how you first perceived relationships. What was your relationship like with your siblings? With your parents? With your friends? With your classmates?

- What traditions and rituals did your family have? What things did you do together (eat dinner, take vacations, play Monopoly)?

- What did you do on Sundays? On Saturdays? In the evenings? On holidays? For vacations?

- What was middle school like? Junior high school? High school?

- When did you feel included? When did you feel left out?

- What were your hobbies? Your interests?

- What were your talents?
- Write about boyfriends and girlfriends.

- Write about your involvement in sports or any honors you received.

- Did you go to college?

- What was your college life like?

- Tell about your work experience.

- Tell about your religious experience (or exposure).

- What do you consider to be your greatest mistake in life?

- What do you consider to be your greatest success?

Encourage your remembrances to go beyond this list. These questions are only intended to jog your memory.

•

It is not our history that molded us;
it's our perception of our history.

•

For some, this will seem a difficult assignment. But you *can* do it. Start with what you do remember. You will be surprised at how much will flood back.

When you've finished writing, take a break and reward yourself for a job well done. You deserve it.

## STEP #2: READ YOUR LIFE STORY ALOUD

It would be easier to read your story silently to yourself, but in such a vital event as this, it is important to have a witness. But choose that witness carefully. It should *not* be:

- someone who will pass judgment or place blame.
- someone who will be compelled to add commentary.
- someone who will second guess your motives.

It *should* be someone who will be willing to simply listen and bear witness to your life as you recall it. That person might be:

- a therapist
- a counselor
- a minister or rabbi
- a doctor
- a school counselor

We strongly suggest that you *not* read it to someone with whom you have a personal relationship, such as a friend or family member. There may well be things in your narrative that a person close to you just cannot handle:

*"You mean you actually slept with that guy? I can't believe you'd do such a stupid thing!*

If it's someone who knew you or your family in the

past, that person may want to correct you:

*"Wait a minute! Mom didn't blame you for that. She blamed me!*

Also, it can put an undue pressure on that other person:

*"Your uncle did WHAT? Well, I'll never again have Thanksgiving with the family if he's at the table!*

And no matter how much you trust that person to keep your confidence, you will never be able to be absolutely sure he or she has done so.

*"Do you swear you didn't tell anyone? Cross-your-heart-hope-to die swear it?*

Some people insist that the safest, most comfortable thing is to just read it out loud alone. But that is not the same. There is no way you can ever be an objective listener to your own life story. If you have no minister or rabbi, you are too old to have a school counselor, your doctor is your sister, and there is no way you could ever afford even one hour with a counselor or therapist, reading *out loud* to yourself is better than nothing. It will allow you to vent your emotions, and you may gain some understanding from hearing the words aloud. But it will never be as effective as having an impartial person listen, bear witness, and affirm that "you are okay."

Depending on how you see God—or a Higher Power—it may be possible to read it aloud to him. If you see God as a loving father who cares and forgives—in our opinion, the true picture of God— then, yes, read it to him. But if God, to you, is a punitive, judgmental authority figure just waiting to zap you over some misdeed, you will only end up feeling more burdened with guilt than ever. You may decide it is best not to share your life story with anyone. That's okay. You can still learn simply by writing it out.

## STEP #3: LISTEN AND LEARN

Be prepared to hear information that is surprising to you even though it is coming from your own memories. It is natural to resist getting new information about yourself, but it will be much easier to hear that information if you have permission to do so. And so we, John DeFoore and Marion Sue Jones, professional therapists who have listened to thousands of life stories read aloud, give you permission to listen and to hear.

•

Accept what you wrote and learn from it.

•

What might you hear? Let's eavesdrop on a couple of people who are hearing new information about themselves.

TED: *"The safest place in my house was in the basement closet under the pile of dirty laundry. Whenever I got in trouble, that's where I hid. If there were no dirty clothes in the basement, I hid outside in the doghouse."*

Here is what Ted learned about himself:

*"If the place I felt safest was under the dirty clothes in the basement or in the doghouse, that tells me a lot about why I spend so much of my time drunk. What can you expect from a person who sees most of his world as unsafe?"*

MARY: *"You want to know when our family all got together? I can answer that in one word—Never! Breakfast was a grab-a-pop-tart-if-you-can affair.*

> *When we ate dinner, the television was always on, and no one talked to anyone else. Afternoons and weekends, everyone went their own way and did their own thing. Dad often didn't get home until I was in bed, and if he did, he parked himself on the couch with the remote control."*

Here is what Mary learned about herself:

> *"Well, I know I have a huge problem forming any kind of intimate relationships. It's scary to me to let people get too close. So now I wonder, could it have to do with the fact that real relationships are unknown to me? I had a mother and a father and a sister and a brother, but there was no unity there. We were a family, but there was no close relationship between us."*

As you read your own life story aloud, keep your ears open. You may be surprised at what you learn.

## STEP #4: LET WHAT YOU LEARN ABOUT YOURSELF MOTIVATE YOU TO CHANGE YOUR LIFE

Linda's father was an alcoholic. Her mother, frustrated and furious, took her anger out on the kids—especially Linda, who was the oldest. Linda was yelled at, scolded, belittled, and cursed. Even as an eighth grader, she was still getting "spankings" that left welts and bruises on her legs. When her father spoke to her, it was to pronounce her a tramp. Somewhere, at some time in her mind, Linda decided, "Fine. Whatever you call me, that's what I am." And that's what she was when she came to see us—a prostitute.

Linda responded to a family situation that was not of her choosing and not of her own making. That's what we all do.

•

A lot of our early choices were made simply because of the circumstances in our lives at the time. And like Linda, to one degree or another, we allow them to form our present lifestyle and our destiny for the future.

•

Look and see if you can identify an event to which you can point and say:

"From that point on, I probably decided I would...
  • ...start...
  • ...stop...
  • ...move closer to...
  • ...move away from...
  • ...protect myself by...

If you have gone this far and you don't see anything, it is likely because you have not yet claimed the permission we spoke of earlier —the permission to learn and be objective about your history. Giving and accepting permission is an important part of good therapy. Decide that you *will* look at your life and that you *will* learn from it.

## STEP #5: TEAR UP YOUR LIFE STORY AND THROW IT INTO THE WASTEBASKET

Your written story has now served its purpose, and it's time to get rid of it. Don't put it into a journal. Don't try to publish it. Don't hide it away to mull over later. It has served its usefulness. Throw it away.

Your life story was your own personal road map to yesterday. But now yesterday is over and gone. This is another day and a new beginning.

•

It's time to start down a new road which will lead to a new future.

•

By physically disposing of your written life record, you will be taking the first step toward discarding your reactions to the injurious material from your past and moving on to write new plans for your future.

Your past is past. What's done is done. You can't change a minute of it. But you can begin a new script for your future.

# 3
## DRAWING YOUR ROAD MAP TO TOMORROW

*"What you're telling me is that I need to learn to put my oxygen mask firmly in place before I start trying to get oxygen masks on the people around me."*

Liz and Joe are desperately in love and are planning to get married. Joe is so romantic. He knows that yellow is Liz's favorite color and that tulips are her favorite flower, so he sees to it that every week, rain or shine, in season or out, Liz has yellow tulips on her desk at work. And Liz loves Joe right back. Even though she's never cared for Italian food ("Too heavy!" she always said), she has learned to make lasagna because it's Joe's favorite dish. Liz lives to make Joe happy, and Joe insists that what makes him happy is making Liz happy.

Ah, love!

Liz and Joe are doing a great job of courting. *Since they never saw their parents at this stage of life, they have no learned script for how a courtship should go.* They just do it their way, and it's working out great.

•

Scripts are predetermined ways of behaving,
"written" for us by someone else.

•

Then they get married, and something clicks in. For this, they do have scripts. From his father (his role model), Joe learned how to act as a husband. And Liz remembers how her mother (her role model) acted as a wife. Marriage they have seen, so as they leave the wedding chapel, they pick up their husband/wife scripts.

Very soon, something starts to happen.

"He's changed," Liz says as she gazes at the empty flower vase on her desk.

"She's changed," Joe laments as he looks at his plate of take-out Chinese food.

Their marriage could probably stand this first scripted impact, but then along comes another: They have a child. Liz stops being a wife and a girlfriend and a fun date and turns into a mother.

"Liz is so involved with the baby, she doesn't have time for me anymore," Joe complains, so he turns his focus to the office. As soon as he gets home, he gives Liz a peck on the cheek, tosses the baby in the air to hear him giggle, then parks himself in front of the television.

Liz's and Joe's romantic, united world is splitting apart. They see it happening. But Joe says, "I have to work hard and make a living for all these people. And I have to relax when I get home." And Liz says, "I'm so busy. And my child needs me!"

•

Liz and Joe are now living a scripted life.

•

Of course, this is a superficial example of determining behavior by the way parents behave. The point is, scripts run deep, and when they are followed they can take a serious toll on our lives. They rob us of being who we uniquely are by causing us to mimic the life of someone from our past. Scripts make us recycle history.

## YOUR LIFE SCRIPT

Engraved on your heart in childhood and authored by the significant people from your early life, *your life script tells you who you are and what you can expect in life*. It tells you of your abilities and capabilities. Only when you understand your life script can you understand your options for growth and change. Only then will you truly understand that you do not have to live at the mercy of your script.

In his book, *Beyond Games and Scripts*,[1] Eric Berne defines the script as: "A life plan based on a decision made in childhood, reinforced by the parents, justified by subsequent events, and culminating in a chosen alternative." Identifying the scripts they are following would help Liz and Joe understand why they are acting the way they are.

Actors know what to say and how to act because it is all written down for them in the script. In much the same way...

•

Each person has a script for
conducting his or her life.

•

It comes from different places and different people, but it centers around parents and home. You yourself actually had little input into your script. You didn't decide

- when you would be born.
- where your birth would take place.
- *if* you would be born at all.
- what sex you would be.
- where you would live.

[1]*Beyond Games and Scripts*, Eric Berne, Grove Press, New York, 1976. Page 350.

- what kind of mother and father you'd have.
- whether or not you would have brothers or sisters.
- anything about any of your relatives.

You had very little, if anything, to say about any of the people who wrote your life script for you. *Yet even today, that old script can determine how you work and play, and how you relate to those close to you—even to the world in general.*

But that can change. It is possible for you to take control. Once you have recognized that old script, you can make decisions about what you want your life to be.

•

You can write a new script.

•

This doesn't mean that the old script is completely gone and will have no further effect on you. Those early influences were deeply etched into your brain. Although the new script can override the old one, the old one will certainly make periodic reappearances. This often happens when a person is under stress, or is tired or sick. It's important to understand it will happen. Expect it, and don't be discouraged when it does. React by recognizing that old script and once again tossing it out.

## RECOGNIZING THE OLD SCRIPT

If you can recognize the old script, you can control it. Unfortunately, this is not as easy as it sounds. Scripts are subtle. They wear deceptive masks. And they cause us to assume our old postures in ways large and small.

To understand how a script works, picture Bob and Ruth settling into their office.

**Bob:**  *"Ruth, do you know what time it is?"*
**Ruth:**  *"Why? Are you saying I'm late?"*

Ruth didn't hear Bob's real question. If she had, she would have said, "Sure, Bob, it's 9:35." What he wanted to know was the position of the long hand and the short hand on the clock. What she *heard* was an echo from her life script: *"You're late again!"*

Your life script causes you to respond to people and situations in a way that has nothing to do with them.

•

Don't underestimate the power of your life script.

•

Amy, a young woman in her 20s, had had two colon surgeries. "These problems are in my family," she explained. "As far back as I can remember, my mother has been telling me that all the women in my family suffer from constipation. And sure enough, it's been a problem for me, too, just like for my mother and my grandmother and my great-grandmother."

Strange thing, though. Despite all that attention on the colon, Amy had never had the principle of digestion explained to her. She knew nothing of the way the intestinal tract naturally moves food through the body. All she had ever heard was that all the women in her family were constipated. The message from Amy's life script was that her body could not function in a normal, healthy way. By recognizing the old script, and by making strategic changes in it, Amy was able to overcome her life-long bowel problems.

Certainly not all medical problems can be handled this way. But some physical problems can indeed be a result of "health scripts."

•

Your script, unexamined and unchallenged,
is a powerful force in determining the
quality of your life.

•

## WRITE OUT A NEW SCRIPT

It's time to write a new script, one based on the here
and now. The following questions will help you begin.

**Part 1:**

My worst childhood experience was when

_____
_____
_____
_____
_____
_____

When that happened, I felt (frustrated, angry, sad, lonely...)

_____
_____
_____

Look at this experience and these feelings with as
much objectivity as you possibly can. If a child had made
decisions about him or herself, the world, and life in general, based just on this little vignette, what would he or she
likely have decided about life?

The child would have decided that life is (dangerous, exciting, frightening, overwhelming...)

_____

_____

_____

What would the child have decided about people? People are (cruel, powerful, unavailable, indifferent, vengeful...)

_____

_____

_____

What would the child decide about him- or herself? I am (not okay, bad, a disappointment, unlovable...)

_____

_____

_____

## Part 2:

My best experience happened when I

_____

_____

_____

_____

_____

_____

When that happened, I felt (excited, elated, loved, accepted...)

_____

_____

_____

Look at this experience and these feelings with as much objectivity as you possibly can. If a child had made decisions about him or herself, the world, and life in general, based just on this little vignette, what would he or she likely have decided about life?

The child would have decided that life is (interesting, exciting, safe, fun...)

_____

_____

_____

What would the child have decided about people? People are (caring, kind, helpful, forgiving...)

_____

_____

_____

What would the child decide about him- or herself? I am (okay, lovable, accepted, appreciated...)

_____

_____

_____

**Part 3:**

As a child, my fantasy was to be (the Lone Ranger, Cinderella, a great dancer....)

_____

_____

My mother's motto for life would be

_____

_____

My father's motto for life would be

_____

_____

How old will you be when you die? (Put down the first figure that comes to your mind.)

_____

_____

How will you die? (heart attack, cancer, car accident)

_____

_____

Who will be with you at the time of your death? (spouse, children, doctors and nurses, no one...)

_____

_____

_____

If you had written an epitaph for yourself that summed up your life on Earth, what would it say? (in 10 words or fewer)

_____

_____

_____

Imagine that six months after you've departed this earth, people are sitting around talking about you. Someone says, "I was out at the cemetery today, and I passed our friend's grave. And guess what, there's no epitaph on the gravestone." So your friends say, "Well, let's write one."

What do you think they would write as an epitaph to your life?

_____

_____

The one thing I think I will never accomplish is

_____

_____

The one thing I am very sure I *will* accomplish is

_____

_____

Look over your answers. Make any changes you wish.

Now read it over once again. Do you see evidences of the script you are currently living out? Are you happy with it?

If, over the course of this book, you do manage to change everything you want to change about yourself, in what ways will you be different?

1. _____

_____

2. _____

_____

3. _____

_____

How will people see you differently?

1. _____

_____

2. _____

_____

3. _____

_____

4. _____

_____

How will they experience you differently?

1. _____

2. _____

3. _____

4. _____

How will life be different for you?

1. _____

2. _____

3. _____

4. _____

How will you see yourself differently?

1. _____

2. _____

3. _____

4. _____

How will you feel differently?

1. _____
   _____

2. _____
   _____

3. _____
   _____

4. _____
   _____

How will you behave differently?

1. _____
   _____

2. _____
   _____

3. _____
   _____

4. _____
   _____

What would you most like to change as a result of this book?

1. _____
   _____

2. _____
   _____

3. _____
   _____

4. _____
   _____

●

There will be times when your old script attacks
and affects your feelings, but you are no longer
under its control.

●

# 4
# MOTHER AND CHILD...FOREVER

*"Mirror, mirror on the wall,
I am my mother after all."*

Don and Barbara were caring for their six-month-old grandson Ryan for the weekend. He was fine for about an hour, but then he seemed to suddenly realize mother and daddy weren't there, and he started crying. Don and Barbara were experienced parents; they raised four kids of their own. But despite their best efforts, little Ryan kept screaming.

"We need help!" Don exclaimed.

A friend's daughter-in-law had a baby almost the same age as Ryan, so in desperation Don called her. "Drop whatever you're doing and come over here right now. We have an emergency!"he said.

She hurried over and immediately saw the problem. She picked the baby up and put him on her shoulder. Instantly Ryan stopped crying. Within minutes he was fast asleep.

How could a friend's daughter-in-law do what two loving grandparents couldn't? Because although she wasn't his mother, she was able to offer the baby a mother's breath, a mother's feel, and a mother's touch.

The special bonding that takes place between the female and the infant is an integral part of the formation and structure of the personality.

The basic personality is formed primarily through the

relationship with the mother. It makes sense. Each one of us, man or woman, was introduced to life by a female. We spent the first nine months of our existence in her body, and she introduced us to life. Her heartbeat was the first sound we heard. Her eyes were the first eyes we saw. Her caress was the first loving touch we felt. Her cooing and nuzzling provided our first feelings of loving acceptance. Long before we could speak, we responded to her through sensory interaction. In addition, most of us spent our childhood primarily under the care of females.

## WHAT A MOTHER COMMUNICATES

Although other females play significant parts, mother is the model for a person's feminine side. This is true for men as well as for women, for all of us have both a feminine side and a masculine side. Along with

- validation
- acceptance
- approval

a healthy feminine parent communicates

- tenderness
- softness
- gentleness
- warmth
- compassion
- empathy.

A mother's contribution has a non-physical, non-mental, nonintellectual dimension that causes it to permeate the very being of the child.

How did your mother

- give you validation in your life?
- show affection?
- *withhold* validation?
- *withhold* affection?

These are important considerations *because they form the model that serves as a template for your relationships with all the other females in your life.*

It is important to understand that most mothers never intentionally deprive their children emotionally. The great majority do the best they can. But for reasons that go back into their own histories, some are not able to give the emotional support their children need.

## SURROGATE MOMS

To some degree, children who grow up under the care of substitute mothers are going to suffer in terms of personality development. That's because no surrogate can ever fully take the place of a healthy mother. At the risk of sounding politically incorrect and stirring up disagreement, we hold fast to this position. For over 30 years, this is what we have consistently heard from clients ("She was good to me, but she wasn't my mother.").

•

Mothers are irreplaceable.

•

What happens when
- the first eyes baby sees are the doctor's eyes?
- baby gets a bottle from whoever happens to be available?
- a baby is raised by childcare workers?

To some degree, that child is going to suffer. There is something in the cuddling that comes along with mother's milk, something in the tender touch of mother's hands, something that can be seen nowhere but in mother's eyes, something that is essential in the formative period of an infant's life.

•

At the start of life, nothing takes
the place of mother.

•

Certainly there are times when, because of circumstances, a mother substitute is necessary. The more caring and nurturing that person is, the better. A loving grandmother is likely a good substitute. A caring, nurturing housekeeper or nanny may be, too.

Infant becomes child, child becomes adolescent, adolescent becomes teen, and teen becomes adult. As the little one grows, a healthy mother, through a series of progressive steps, separates herself from her child.

*But healthy separation does not always happen.*

**For a Daughter...**

There are several unhealthy dynamics that define separation problems between a mother and daughter. Here are some common ones:

**1. Too-Attractive Mama**

The Too-Attractive Mama is so lovely and glamorous her daughter feels she can never measure up. Or if she can, she had better not, because that would threaten her mother's identity. This is especially true if physical beauty is an obsession with the mother.

## 2. Second-Chance Mom

This mother doesn't really have—or never did have—a life of her own. She experiences excitement in her life by living through her daughter. She pushes her daughter to be popular, insists she be a cheerleader or the homecoming queen. She is willing to sacrifice anything to have her daughter in the right school, dating the right boys, wearing the right clothes, in the right sorority. When the time comes, she wants her daughter to marry the "right" man. And she expects something back for her "sacrifices"—she wants the life she wasn't able to live herself.

Another type of Second-Chance Mom believes she compromised her own life by marrying. Maybe she wishes she could have had a profession and have "made something of myself." She often feels at the mercy of her husband. So she insists to her daughter, "You do what I didn't do. Don't waste your life like I did. Get a career so you don't have to depend on a man!"

## 3. Put-Down Mother

This type of mother elevates herself by criticizing and belittling her daughter. "I don't know why you would do such a stupid thing!"she exclaims. Or, "Your hair is stringy. Why don't you do something with it?" Or, "Don't stuff your face. You're already too fat." The problem is not the daughter; it is the mother's feelings of inferiority that come out in put-downs and criticism. The result? A sense of inferiority and despair—a sense of being unacceptable—within her daughter.

## 4. Super-Duper Mom

The Super-Duper Mom is very bright, very successful, very accomplished, very everything. Convinced she can never measure up to mom, daughter doesn't even try. She sees herself as a loser and gives up without a battle. Once the daughter of a Super-Duper Mom realizes she can never achieve what her mother does, she often turns in the opposite direction and picks losers for associates, confidants, and friends. She runs with the losing crowd, and dresses the part. This is the very thing her mother cannot tolerate.

A Super-Duper Mom doesn't let her daughter think for herself. Mom makes the decisions on clothes, hairstyle, activities. She does the girl's homework ("How else will my daughter get an A?"). She solves all her daughter's problems. There is no concern about financial responsibility, because "Mom will take care of it for you."

### 5. Backseat-Driver Mother

At first look, Backseat-Driver Mother seems quiet, willing to let father be in the driver's seat. He is likely forceful, stubborn, unbending and unwilling to back down. It's only on careful examination that mother emerges as the behind-the-scenes manipulator. When mother is upset with daughter, she conveys it to father, and he takes over. That way, father is the "bad guy," not her. Her forte is pitting father and daughter against each other. Although she keeps the two stirred up, she never *seems* to be involved.

This kind of mother may actually be fearful of losing her place with her husband. A threatened mother is an insecure mother. As a result of her insecurity, she protects her place by faulting the daughter and alienating daughter and father. All the time her daughter is struggling to make her mother happy, and it cannot be done.

### For a Son...

There are also unhealthy dynamics that define separation problems between mother and son. Here are some of them:

### 1. Hang-On Mom

The Hang-On Mom attaches herself to her son, and out

of her own neediness for affection and companionship puts him into the position of special confidant. She may not have a spouse, or her spouse may be physically or emotionally absent. Her son, usually just a child, ends up hearing her problems, her needs, her confidences —things he doesn't have the maturity to handle. She goes to him for the affection, approval, or comfort she so desperately needs. *In effect, she turns her son into a spouse.* The boy is not prepared emotionally for this spousal role, and it can cripple him.

Mother does her utmost to keep her son a child. When he grows into manhood, any woman he looks at as a possible wife is— according to mom—the wrong woman. She just cannot let him go. And this son often ends up agreeing not to grow up.

## 2. Rejecting Mother

There are mothers who—because of their own histories of intimidation, or being taken advantage of, or put down by their own male role models—have developed a dislike, or even a hatred, of men. The older the son gets, the more apparent the Rejecting Mother's feelings become. She takes her own anger and hatred for men and projects it onto her son. She rejects him and rejects him and rejects him. She puts him down and puts him down and puts him down. She criticizes and criticizes and criticizes—all justified in her mind. She does everything she can to emotionally castrate her son.

Keep in mind that *none of these things was done intentionally*. In fact, they might not have happened at all. What has such a profound effect on us is our *childhood perception* of what happened, and it may or may not be accurate. Of one thing we can be sure:

•

There are no perfect mothers or fathers.

•

All parents have needs. All carry scars from wounds they suffered as children. It is when parents are unaware of their own issues, however, that they unwittingly and unintentionally attempt to use their children to fill the holes or rectify the scars in their own lives.

## SAY GOOD-BYE TO MAMA

It is time to say good-bye to those old destructive patterns of behavior—to the mother-child dependencies. Separate from your childhood mama so that you can become a separate, whole human being in your own right. You can do this even if your mother is no longer living.

Greg and Anne, coming back from Europe with a group of twelve people they had taken on a three-week study tour, landed at La Guardia airport in New York in the middle of a raging January blizzard. It was so bad that their plane was the last one allowed to land before the final runway was closed down.

Throughout childhood it was drilled into Anne that you don't spend money unless you absolutely have to. You make do. Here's how the exchange went as Greg and Anne led the others to a distant terminal:

Greg:     *"It's freezing out here! Let's get a cab."*
Anne:     *"A cab! It would be foolish to pay all that money for a cab. We can get the shuttle for 50 cents. It will be by any minute."*
Greg:     *"But it may take a while. It's snowing like crazy, and I'm cold!"*
Anne:     *"It'll be here in just a minute. We can wait."*

*The whole group huddled together on the curb, struggling to keep from freezing. It was snowing so hard that Anne pulled her coat up over her head. Ten or fifteen minutes passed—it seemed like hours. Cabs zipped past regularly.*

Greg:     *"Why don't we catch a cab?"*

Anne:    *"The shuttle will be here in a minute. It's only 50 cents."*

*They waited a few more minutes. Finally Greg had had enough.*

Greg:     *"You do what you want. I'm getting a cab."*

*He stepped off the curb, and a cab stopped immediately. The minute he opened the door, everyone piled in—including Anne who almost crowded Greg out!*

*As they pulled away, crammed in and piled on top of each other, Anne mumbled, "My father would die if he saw us spending money for a cab!"*

*The cab driver turned around and said, "So would mine, lady. So would mine!*

That wasn't Anne standing there on the curb making a decision that day. Anne was freezing, and she could well afford a cab. Rather, it was the parent in her head saying, "Don't spend money on a cab! You can stand there and wait for the shuttle. For Pete's sake, a cab is a waste of ten dollars! Do you think money grows on trees?"

Greg saw what Anne couldn't see. "It's what made me stop the taxi," he said. "I looked over there, and under the coat Anne had draped over her head to keep the snow off, I saw her father's face."

Anne's parents had struggled through the Depression and war times. For them, it was wise to save every penny. Scrimping was a survival mode. The problem came when...

•

Anne failed to update that information
to her own life and circumstances.

•

Saying good-bye to the past:

- It begins with a conscious decision that from this moment on, you will be in charge of your life.
- You will give respect to what your mother taught you. You will give it a hearing. You will stop and evaluate it.
- Then you will decide whether or not it is best for you today.

What your mother did, and what she taught you, may have been exactly right for her at that time, in that place. But it may not be at all right for you today.

•

Saying good-bye is an ongoing process.

•

## GOOD-BYE OR HELLO?

Saying good-bye to the old child-mama dynamics means saying hello to a new adult-adult dynamic. No longer will you need to adapt to or rebel against your mother. No longer will it be your responsibility to make her happy, or to placate her, or to irritate and rebel against her.

A good way to say good-bye is to actually write a good-bye letter to your mother. *BUT: Do not give this letter to your mother!* After it is written and read out loud, tear it up and throw it away. This is not the mother you talk to on the telephone on Sundays and drive to the grocery store and send flowers to on Mother's Day.

•

The letter is for the mother in your head who will not allow you to grow up and operate as an autonomous adult.

•

The mother in your head is the one you knew 10 or 20 or 30 years ago, an image of authority you have constructed and held on to.

In this letter, tell your mother

- how life with her was for you, both positive and negative.
- what happened to you as a result.
- what it is you are changing today.

You might want to begin by saying something such as:

*I know you did the best you could with what you had at the time. Thank you for all the good things you've given me and done for me. I forgive you for all your mistakes.*

*I do want to tell you what it was like being in a relationship with you.* (Then tell her.)

*This has created a problem for me.* (Tell her what that problem is.)

*As a result of that relationship, here is what is happening in my life.* (Lay it out for her.)

*Since I am now an adult, I want you to know that from now on I assume responsibility for my life, for my behavior, and for the consequences of my decisions.*

No longer can you say, "Well, I probably do that just because my mother.... It's her fault."

From now on, the buck stops with you.

But how about father? We'll talk about him in the next chapter.

•

At this point, you transfer the authority you formally gave your mother from your mother to yourself... and you take charge of your own life.

•

# 5
# FATHER AND CHILD...FOR NEVER

*"There is no such thing as constructive criticism. If criticism were constructive, we'd all be perfect by now."*

Darren, the baby of the family, was spoiled rotten by his mother. Even she admits that she might have gone too far—cleaning his room, cutting up his meat, scolding anyone who offended him. Darren's brother and sister—11 and 12 years old when he was born—always resented the way their mother babied him. By the time he was in high school, his father began to worry.

"Son," he said, "I've rented a cabin in the woods. We're going to go up there, just you and me, and *really be men!*"

They spent the week with dad pushing Darren to hunt, fish, drink beer, and play poker like a man. Darren hated it. When they got home, Darren complained bitterly to his mother, and she made him hot cocoa with marshmallows and babied him more than ever.

"I give up!" his father said. "He's hopeless! That boy will *never* be a real man!"

Carl Jung, the distinguished Swiss psychiatrist, taught that we carry within us the same seeds of thought and feelings as did our ancient ancestors. The man who leaves home today for the morning commute, armed with briefcase and *Wall Street Journal*, is on the inside the same man who thousands of years ago crept out of his cave with a stone axe. Today's man goes to the factory, the work site, or the office; yesterday's man went out into the jungle to hunt the mastodon. More alike than different, both men have the same feelings, passions, drives, and instincts. Today's man may be somewhat more refined, but his basic identity has not been altered.

## FATHER'S INFLUENCE

Your father's influence on you was not as definitive in shaping your personality as was your mother's. Although our politically correct side doesn't like it, to be intellectually honest we have to admit that when God set in motion this eternal scheme of things, he gave the mother a role in shaping and forming the child's personality that he didn't entrust to the father. Even so, both parents are extremely important. Rather than *duplicating* influence, mother and father *complement* one another.

A father influences his child in areas of:

- safety
- affirmation
- validation
- logic
- encouragement
- establishment of boundaries
- limit setting
- aggression.

It was from your father that you got the majority of your masculine side.

## YOUR MASCULINE SIDE

The masculine side comes primarily from your father, although you get a certain part of it from the masculine side of your mother. The father models to the son how to be a man, *but the mother must give him permission to be a man*. The mother shows the daughter how to be a woman, but the *father must give her permission to be a woman*.

**To his Daughter, a Father...**

...is a pattern for all her future relationships with the opposite sex. When her masculine side is not developed, she doesn't know how to protect and take care of herself. This is true physically, but it goes far beyond that. She is also vulnerable mentally, emotionally, financially, and socially. Often women who have poorly developed masculine sides don't have the internal permission to think, to figure things out, to be logical. We know such women as "helpless females" who make such statements as:
- I don't know what to do when little red lights come on in the car."
- "I just can't balance my checkbook. He earns the money and I spend it."
- "I never understood mechanical stuff."

These are the women who, because of their dependency, allow themselves to be manipulated, controlled, even abused by men.

On the other hand, women who have strong masculine sides tend to be aggressive, objective, logical, and to think in terms of function and the big picture. Were a man to attempt to take advantage of such a woman, she would be insulted and indignant, and would put an immediate stop to it.

•

The quality of acceptance a father gives his daughter carries with it a validation of her female identity and her feminine side.

•

This gives her a preview of what she can, or should, expect from men.

•

A father's relationship with his daughter sets the stage for her future interaction and relationships with men.

•

When she sees how he relates to her mother, it tells her how she should expect men to relate to her. When she sees how he relates to her, it reinforces it.

The lesson may be a positive one of love or trust or dependability, or it may be a negative one of inability or distrust or being a second class person. Most often, a woman who sees herself as a colleague, on an equal footing with men, was given that status by her father's respect for her as she entered adulthood.

There are several unhealthy dynamics we see between fathers and daughters. Some common ones are:

### 1. Too Busy To Be Bothered Father

The neglectful father has many places to go and important things on his mind. When he's home, he "has the right to relax in front of the television set." So what's the problem?

The problem is that the daughter of such a father grows up expecting to be neglected by men. Even if she isn't neglected, she thinks she is, because that's the pattern she's used to. In fact, she sees any attention from a man as suspect.

## 2. Doting "Daddy's Little Girl" Father

The privileged "Daddy's Little Girl" is adored by her father and he devotes himself to her. Problems arise when a doting daddy never tells his little girl "no," doesn't set appropriate boundaries, doesn't call her to be responsible, or is not being an appropriate parent. A responsible father is one who is willing to look and listen, and if need be to say, "No, you can't do that. I love you and support you, but that's not an option."

In his eyes, Daddy's Little Girl can do no wrong. And since she projects her daddy's image onto whatever man comes into her life, she grows up watching and waiting for Prince Charming to burst in, to solve all her problems, and to provide her with instant happiness forever.

In effect, *Daddy's Little Girl refuses to grow up.* She is never really able to accept responsibility as an adult, or to consider herself equal to men. So she often looks for an older man to marry. He dotes on her while they are courting, and treats her just like her daddy did. But after they get married, when it becomes clear that she's not about to grow up, things often go sour. She continues to operate like a little girl, resisting and resenting and wanting to be catered to and protected.

## 3. Abusive Father

Although Tina's father never physically abused his family, he certainly had a violent temper. Tina grew up cowering in fear during her father's terrifying explosions. By the time she was in her third year of college, smart, popular, attractive Tina had everything going for her. So who was she dating? Sam, a huge guy with a violent temper just like dad's, but with a terrifying twist: he was also physically abusive. We saw Tina after Sam had dragged her by her hair out of her apartment, down the hall, and into the parking lot where he beat her badly enough to blacken both her eyes, break her nose, and fracture her arm.

"But I love him, and I know he loves me," Tina insisted. "Okay, he got too rough with me. He admits it. But he's not always like that."

Raised by a hot-tempered, screaming father and a placating, peace-at-any-cost mother, *Tina's masculine side had never developed*. When a woman doesn't have her masculine side strengthened by a healthy and positive exposure to her father, and her mother doesn't have a strong masculine side to compensate, it's easy for the woman to give her power and authority over to a man.

"But any woman can fall in with the wrong guy and end up abused," some argue.

"Fall in" with the wrong guy? No. End up beaten? No. End up *abused*? Absolutely not. Women with a strong masculine side aren't abused. They can and do take care of themselves.

## 4. Daddy's Partner

This is the dynamic that occurs when daddy confides in his daughter instead of in his wife. It may be because mother is not available physically (as in a single parent dad), or—as is more often the case—because she is emotionally unavailable. It's common for such a daughter to proudly claim, "Daddy and I could talk about *everything*, and we did!"But this is not an appropriate father-daughter relationship. It is more appropriate for a husband and wife. Such a father is inviting his daughter to be like a wife to him.

Daddy's Partner daughters find it very difficult to leave daddy and get married. That's not surprising; really, in a perverse way, she's already married.

## 5. Daddy's Little Boy

This role usually falls to a daughter whose father has no son. He takes her with him into his man's world: they hunt, fish, play ball. Certainly there is nothing wrong with a girl doing any or all of these things. Nor is there anything unhealthy about her dad doing them with her. It becomes a problem when there is no reinforcement by dad of her feminine world. Father is relating to her only on his turf. Keeping her mainly in a man's world reinforces the girl's place as "the little boy daddy never had."

## To his Son, a Father...

...models how to, or how not to, be a man. Like girls, boys have to separate themselves from their mothers, but unlike girls, boys have to claim an entirely different form of sexuality.

•

A boy desperately needs a father to model masculinity for him.

•

It is through his dad that the boy finds his place in the community, in society, and in the world at large. The social adaptability of a boy is tied to the validation he gets from his father.

Here are some of the dynamics we see between father and son:

## 1. Super Successful Dad

When the father is very successful or very accomplished, a son can feel that he will never be able to measure up to dad. He sees dad as being above and beyond anything he could ever achieve. Dad may even compete with the son if he feels insecure about his place as a man.

## 2. Househusband Papa

It is becoming more and more common to see families where the mother earns more than the father, so she is the one who works outside the home and the father is the one who stays home and cares for the kids. Certainly it's good to have a loving parent at home, but is the father the best one for infants and very young children? We don't think so. Househusband Papas can be very nurturing and loving, but however hard they try, they cannot be mothers, just as women cannot be fathers. In the typical role reversal, something seems to be lost in the feminine and masculine teaching.

Take Adam, for instance. He is the father of four children. Several years ago his wife informed him that she was in love with someone else and was leaving him and the children. Mom's new husband has no interest in the kids—in fact, he complains about every penny she spends on them. Adam has custody, and he does his best to compensate for the mother who left. The kids love and respect their daddy, yet they also love their mother. In a hundred different ways they beg for her affection and attention. Often, on her appointed day to have them, she never shows up. Yet the children sit and wait patiently. They long for a mother's love.

That's not to say there isn't a profoundly important relationship that takes place between child and father. *The father's role is equally important.* But it is a different role.

### 3. Absent Father

It's hard for an absent father to be a real dad. He's never around.

"But I want my children to have everything I never had when I was growing up," he insists. So he works longer and longer hours. His children have all the toys and privileges he can possibly provide. What they don't have is dad's presence and attention.

Who of us wants things instead of relationships?

### 4. Passive Papa

Unlike the absent father, Passive Papa is around physically. Problem is, he doesn't model strength and integrity to his son, nor does he model a healthy marriage relationship, one between equals. He is dominated by his wife; she controls the family.

A boy raised by a passive father may follow the example and also be passive. Or he may grow angry and decide: "No one will ever control me like she controls him!"

## 5. Authoritarian Father

The authoritarian father's word is law in the family. There is no discussing or questioning. Domineering, rigid, and unrelenting, he doesn't pick his battles; he has to win them all. He doesn't develop relationships; he runs a business with an empirical attitude! When his son grasps the fact that he is never going to win against dad, he is likely to rebel. He may do this in an overt, confrontational way, or he may go underground where he won't get caught and do it subversively.

## BYE-BYE DAD

To see the importance of the father in the life of a family, we need only look at what has happened between the Industrial Revolution and today. The autonomy and integrity that was prevalent in the American male before the Industrial Revolution has, for the most part, disappeared. Before that time, most men were farmers. They worked in the fields around the house. The family worked together, ate together, and spent evenings and other time away from work together. The Industrial Revolution changed all that. Suddenly the man left an agrarian society for an industrial society. No longer was father in constant contact with the family and family life as he had been on the farm. Now his workplace—the factory —was far away, and he only came home at the end of the day (if he was lucky. It may not have been until the end of the week). No longer did the children have frequent exposure to their male parent. Instead of a constant part of family life, he represented dollars and discipline ("You just wait until your father gets home!").

That's what we see today: *male parents who play secondary roles in the shaping and forming of their children's personalities.* The sad result is that sons don't know how to be men. They have little or no time with their partners. They know how to be mothers, because they grow up watching what mothers do, observing how mothers operate, seeing how mothers interact with people. Many sons today have mothers as their models—and most of their teachers are female as well.

•

Too often, boys know how to be women,
but they don't know how to be men.

•

Most boys don't have enough exposure to their fathers to get the development, structure, and direction their personalities need to mature. Instead, boys learn to be men only through competitive relationships with their peers.

Yet boys who see their dads even on this limited basis are far better off than those who grow up without a father at all, a situation that is becoming more and more common in our society. Because they have no dads with whom to relate, fatherless boys build for themselves fantasy fathers. Fatherless boys glean ideas from sports heroes, from books they read, television shows and movies they see, computer games they play, and media figures, good and bad. From these, they create fathers for themselves.

Apart from abuse, even a poor parent who is present is of more value to the child than a fantasy parent the child creates. Just take a look at the typical father in the media today. At best he is a comical character. From a one-liner jerk to a fumbling bumbler who occasionally comes out with pearls of wisdom, he is out of touch with his family. *According to the media, the male in today's American family is a joke.*

Many fathers would love to have more time with their families. In fact, there is a trend in some areas for men to willingly cut back on their work time just so that they can have more time at home. So don't automatically look upon dad as the villain here. Mother may have wanted a nice house with lovely furniture. She needed a new car. She wanted private school for the children, and summer camps, and this-and-that lessons. Oh, and don't forget stylish clothes. They're expensive, but ...

Oftentimes dad was doing exactly what he thought he was supposed to be doing: trying to keep his family happy.

"It's really, really hard to be a good father," one man stated. "Everyone in the family had a want list for me, and it all cost money. The harder I worked, the more hours I was away from home. The more I was away, the more my wife tried to fill both her shoes and mine. Day by day, week by week, my family excluded me more and more, until finally I was a stranger in my own home. My family didn't know me and I didn't know them. Nobody meant for it to be that way." After a pause he added, "I allowed it to happen. Nobody did it to me. I accepted it as just how it was."

## AND SO...

The removal of dad has many ramifications, both for our families and for our society.

**For a son, it can mean:**

- He is dependent, unable to take charge.
- He takes on a substitute for the dependence he used to have on mother (such as substance abuse, work, activities, even religion).

- He doesn't know how to form a relationship with his wife.

- He doesn't know how to form a relationship with his children.

- Like his father, he removes himself from the family.

- In order to escape that old role with which he is so uncomfortable, he begins to work compulsively.

**For a daughter, it can mean:**

- She will find herself awkward and intimidated around men.

- She will not be able to see herself as an equal to men.

- A sense of inadequacy may cause her to be "boy crazy," always searching for or clinging to or looking for affection from the boys.

- She may be sexually promiscuous, ever seeking the reassurance and acceptance of a man, and the attention she never got from her father.

- In marriage, she may be angry and resentful. She may simply give up on men, figuring, "Who needs them?"

- When she looks for a mate, her tendency will be to find someone just like dear old dad—never there for her.

## GOOD-BYE AGAIN

As you did with your mother, you need to say good-bye to your father. Again, begin with a decision to no longer give authority for your life over to him. Determine to evaluate your behavior and your decisions in light of who you are today. Then, because this is an ongoing process, *determine to keep updating your thinking, your assumptions, and your behavior.*

Again, we are not saying all the messages you received from or about your father were bad. What we are saying is that they may well be out of date and inappropriate for who you are here and now. Also, since those messages were your impression of what you thought you heard from your father, they do not necessarily reflect his intentions.

## ONE FINAL WORD

In the 30 years we have been in practice, no parent has ever come to us and said, "I got married and decided: I'm going to see what I can do to mess up my kids." *No one ever sets out to be a bad parent.* What they do, they do with the best of intentions. *Most parents did the best they could with what they had at the time.* That's probably what you have done if you are a parent, and it's probably what your children will do with their children.

Look backward long enough to understand your past. Recognize the significant events and persons, and how they impacted you. Evaluate. Update. Say good-bye. Then move on into the present and live there.

•

The place to begin is with the face in your mirror.

•

# 6
# THE FACE IN THE MIRROR

*"Spend your time and energy making plans for yourself."*

Under "describe yourself," a woman we'll call Jeanine wrote: *"Fat, lazy bum."*

Jeanine is a well-paid, highly prized legal secretary, employed by one of the most prestigious law firms in her area. At 45, she is attractive, fit, and dresses extremely well. Fat? No. Lazy? Absolutely not! Why, then, did she describe herself that way? Because, since childhood, that's how she has seen herself.

## THE IMAGE INSIDE YOU

As a little child, everything you knew about life (the people in it and how to interact with them) you learned from your mother and father. The day you were born you started watching, listening, feeling, and reacting, and you never stopped throughout your growing up years. As far as you knew, your mother and father controlled your entire existence: they decided what food you ate, where and when you slept, what you wore—they even controlled the air you breathed. Your very survival depended on them.

•

You made a decision about your worth and importance based on how you felt your mother and your
father felt about you.

•

That doesn't mean Jeanine's parents *told* her she was
fat and lazy. It's much more than just the words parents
say to their child. It's their tone of voice, their gestures,
their body language, the way they touch one another, and
the looks they give their child and each other. It's also what
they valued and what they gave their attention to.

Before you were three years old, you pulled all this
input together, and from it you made an extremely important decision about yourself:

•

You determined your own worth and value
as a person.

•

You may have decided you were extremely important.
You may have decided you were a bother to everyone
around you. You may have decided you were the greatest
thing in the world. Jeanine decided she was fat and lazy,
and not worth much.

Whether you decided you were absolutely wonderful,
or that you were "a fat, lazy bum," *the decision was made
through the eyes of a child*. It was almost certainly erroneous. After all, back then you didn't have the maturity to
evaluate information.

Also, you were occupied with a world of stimuli. Even
though you were only three years old, you had to begin
figuring out how to cope in the world. You looked at your
mother and you decided, *"That's what all women are like."*
You looked over at your father and you decided, *"That's*

*what all men are like.*" And even though you were far too young to have a word for marriage, you watched the two of them and how they related to each other, and you decided what marriage was like.

What you programmed into your internal computer at that tender age formed the information bank from which you will draw for the rest of your life. Back then, you were busy getting your value system set.

•

In fact, by the time you were five years old, approximately 75% of your personality was in place.

•

Not unchangeable, but in place.

When you left home for school, you took your self-image out into the world with you. If you were treated like a king at home, and then everyone at school didn't think you were so all-fired important, you wondered, *"What's wrong here? They aren't treating me right!"* If you felt like you were a nuisance and a bother, that's how you acted in the classroom and on the playground. Like all of us, you imposed your self-image onto the people around you, and that began to set. People treated you the same way you perceived that your parents treated you. If others didn't fit into your mold, you didn't allow them into your life.

That's true even if you didn't *like* the way your parents treated you. We all go back to the feelings that are familiar to us. It's the only way we know to cope. That's because familiar habits are so often misinterpreted as healthy. We habitually repeat patterns that are "safe," whether or not they are productive and healthy.

At about the age of ten or eleven, you made the *second* most important decision of your life:

•

Based on how secure you perceived the relationship between you and your parents to be, you determined your internal security.

•

You have carried these two subconscious decisions—your selfesteem and your internal security—with you into your adult life. No matter what you accomplish, regardless of how well you do socially or financially, no matter how many awards and accolades you accumulate, if those decisions amounted to insecurity, you will still feel insecure. *The image you carry around in your heart or mind is as real to you as the picture on your driver's license.*

Your self-image was set by the time you reached puberty. Yet it is constantly being refined and validated by the ongoing relationships in your life. Unless you are a growing, changing human being, and unless you are constantly updating yourself, whenever people look at you, what they are seeing is a life run by a child of three or four or five.

## NO PERFECT PARENTS

Because no parent is perfect, few of us arrive at adulthood with an accurate image of who we are. But some children, because of their circumstances, have a particularly difficult time accepting an accurate image of themselves.

## "LATCHKEY KIDS"

A troubling and ever growing situation in our society is children we refer to as "latchkey kids." In the past, these were children whose parents both had to work in order to buy food and pay the rent, or they were the children of single parents. This is still the case for many children, but more and more their ranks include the children of upwardly mobile, middle-class parents. Either way, these kids are basically left to fend for themselves. They come home from school and let themselves into the house with their "latchkeys," and they are left to supervise themselves until someone comes home after work. Rather than being nurtured and guided and supervised by their parents, these kids have to manage for themselves.

## SUBSTITUTE CARE

How about children who are in the care of a care provider such as a babysitter, housekeeper, or nanny?

It is better than having kids come home to an empty house, but the fact is, that person is just a substitute. The parent's voice, touch, everyday modeling of values, loving encouragement—the parent's *presence*—is not there.

Parents argue: "But I give my kids everything. They have a good home in a wonderful neighborhood, an excellent school, a new computer, and all kinds of stuff."

Stuff, yes. *But family is basically a sensory experience.* It's not intellectual, not cognitive, not spiritual, not emotional. It's sensory. It has to do with sight, hearing, taste, touch, and smell. If the child is not

- touched
- listened to
- heard
- smelled
- caressed

by a parent—the most significant person in his or her

life—*there is a void in the shaping and forming of that child's personality*. And where there is a void, the child will search for something to fill it. And that alternate source might well be an unhealthy source.

For a child, nothing can take the place of knowing that the most important person on earth to him or her—Mother—is there. Hopefully she

- cares for
- validates
- affirms
- caresses
- touches
- loves
- compliments that child.

And the second most important person—Father—is around to

- affirm
- validate
- encourage
- complement mother's nurturing.

When those two are both absent for the major portion of a child's day, the child continues to search for something to take the place of that nurturing and validation. In the end, the child can come to the conclusion that "*something is wrong with me.*"

Often, when children who miss out on nurturing become adults, they don't know how to nurture themselves. So they subconsciously try to find a substitute. Here are some common ones:

- buying things
- doing things

- staying busy
- being constantly entertained
- being financially irresponsible
- getting sick (hypochondria)
- pursuing addictive choices

## SURROGATE PARENTS

Surrogate parents are all those caring schoolteachers, concerned family members, neighbors, volunteers and youth workers—and just caring people—who have stepped in and saved the emotional lives of so many children and young people. Most of us can point to more than one caring adult we know of who saw a needy child and took the time and effort to make a difference in that young person's life.

When it comes to parents, however imperfect a hand you were dealt, you don't have to play it. You can ask for another deal.

•

You have the ability to parent yourself.

•

You can change that face in the mirror anytime you choose.

In their book on redecision,[2] Bob and Mary Goulding go to the heart of the matter. You can begin to build a new self-image for yourself, one that is all about *you*. And it is

---

[2]*Changing Lives Through Redecision Therapy*, Goulding and Goulding. Bruner/Mazel, 1979.
Bob and Mary Goulding gave new hope to mankind in their teachings on the power of decisions. These two great teacher/therapists brought, and continue to bring, hope and health to those whose lives they touch.

based on *fact* rather than on erroneous assumptions. It will be your basis for making life-long changes in your life.

## THE NEW DECISION

You said good-bye to your mother and father. You said goodbye to your position as their child. You recognized that they did the best they could with what they had at the time. Now it's your turn to take over.

Dwelling in the past produces guilt. Dwelling on the future produces fear. *But living in the present contributes to a different past and changes the future.* So let's move into the present.

Here is the new decision:

•

God (as I understand him) loves me.
Therefore, I love myself.
Then with the love God gives me,
I love God in return.
Therefore, I am okay as I am,
who I am, here and now.

•

This is how it works:

## STEP #1: GOD LOVES ME

The love of a human being can be manipulated. But you cannot manipulate God's love. Human love can be affected by behavior, thoughts, or feelings. God's love cannot be affected by anything. Human beings love *when* and *if* and *because*.

•

## God loves!! Period.

•

Your true value and worth are based on who you are to God—whatever you understand God to be—rather than how you thought your parents felt about you. And your new internal security is based on your relationship with God rather than on your parents. Rather than being in an external relationship with another human being, your value, worth and internal security become an inside job.

You are totally acceptable, totally approved, and totally validated by the Creator of the Universe.

Look at this affirmation and read it out loud:

> *I am loved by God regardless of who else may or may not love me. I am okay even though everyone is not going to like me. Some will and some won't, but who I am is not based on that. My acceptance and my place in this world do not turn on that hinge. I am okay with God. I am okay with myself.*

Read it again, then again. Make a copy of it to hang on the mirror in your bathroom so you will see it first thing every morning and last thing every night. Make another copy to carry in your wallet so you can pull it out and read it whenever you need to be affirmed.

If you don't believe in God, say *"my higher power"* or whatever you feel comfortable with. The important thing is to recognize that you are loved and affirmed by a force of great authority outside yourself. Here, then, is the place to start:

•

## God loves me.

•

## STEP #2: THEREFORE, I LOVE MYSELF

A client we'll call Suzanne had an especially hard time getting through this second step. The words went in her ears, but then they seemed to hit a brick wall. She was an ordinary looking woman in her early 40s, except that she dressed in a particularly unattractive way. You would never notice her in a crowd of two. Her clunky brown shoes were badly scuffed and run-down at the heels. Her shapeless dress hid her tiny waist and attractive figure. And her hair was limp and scraggly. Her appearance had nothing to do with money; she had a good job and a sizable bank account. It had everything to do with her inability to love herself.

After a lot of preliminary work, Suzanne was counseled, "Go to that nice store in the shopping center and buy yourself something soft and pretty."

Suzanne thought of this excuse and that excuse why she couldn't go, but her instructions were firm. Finally Suzanne went, but after just a few minutes in the store, she started to cry. Embarrassed, she ran out.

"I couldn't do it," Suzanne exclaimed. "I looked around at all those beautiful things, but they were far too nice for me. I have no business wearing anything so beautiful."

See how deeply entrenched a self-image can be? Even so, you cannot move past this step until you are able to love yourself.

It is our contention that making yourself as lovely as you can will help you to love yourself. Don't you feel especially good about yourself when you're dressed up, your hair nicely done, makeup on (or freshly shaved)? Doesn't it bring you a little closer to being able to love yourself?

When we wear tacky clothes because "no one will see me," we are saying: *I do care what other people think about me, but I don't care about what I think about myself.*

Here are some statements that can encourage you to

love yourself:

- I was created by God.
- God makes no mistakes.
- God makes no junk.
- I am all right with God as I am, who I am, here and now.
- God is still working on me. He is not finished with me yet.
- God loves me, therefore I love myself.

And because I love myself:

- I will give my body adequate and nourishing food.
- I will rest eight hours a day.
- I will exercise and play regularly.
- I will dress as attractively as I can.
- I will provide a safe and attractive home for myself.
- I will not injure or endanger my physical safety—accidentally or on purpose.
- I will not poison my body with drugs or alcohol.

The second step:

•

Therefore, I love myself.

•

## STEP #3: WITH THE LOVE GOD GIVES ME, I LOVE GOD IN RETURN

I love God with the love he gives me. The love I experience can then overflow and touch others.

You don't even have to provide the love, for it comes

from God. All you have to do is accept it. If you don't believe this, act as if you do, and just watch yourself change and grow. Having a relationship with the Creator of the Universe gives an eternal dimension to the relationship; it automatically puts you in touch with infinity.

The assurance of the third step, then, is:

•

With the love God gives me, I love God in return.

•

## STEP #4: THEREFORE, I AM OKAY AS I AM, WHO I AM, HERE AND NOW

Your worth and value have been established on this earth, and it's not up to question. It's your birthright. You do not have to do anything to earn your worth and value. You don't have to achieve anything, you don't have to live up to anyone else's expectations to have worth and value. It was given to you at birth, and now you can claim it. That's what we mean when we say "I'm okay." I may not be okay with you. I may not be okay with a lot of people. But I'm okay with myself, and I'm okay with God, and that's what matters.

The last step assures:

•

Therefore, I am okay as I am, who I am,
here and now.

•

Here again is the all-important new decision:

*I am loved by God regardless of who else may
or may not love me. I am okay even though*

*everyone is not going to like me. Some will and some won't, but who I am is not based on that. My acceptance and my place in this world do not turn on that hinge. I am okay!*

If you are diligent, the consistent repetition of this affirmation will overpower the old "script" voices from your past.

# 7
# THE VOICE IN THE HEAR-ER

*"I am responsible, I'm not guilty.
I am accountable, I'm not to blame."*

"Mom!" *It was Justin on the telephone calling from his college dorm room.* "I have a paper due for my literature class, and I didn't get around to reading the books. I need you to help me out."

"Again, Justin?" *his mother exclaimed in frustration.* "I have done three papers for you this semester!"

"I know, Mom, but there's just too much work to do. I can't keep up with it all."

"Where were you last night? I called to remind you that you had a tennis clinic today and I got your answering machine."

"Oh, man, I forgot all about the clinic! I was at a basketball game. You should have called back!"

Justin was never taught to be responsible for his behavior. When he was a child and he didn't take care of his toys, his mom and dad bought him new ones. When he kept his library books out too long, his mom returned them for him, along with the overdue payment. In high school, he got speeding tickets and his dad paid them. On his eighteenth birthday, Justin got a citation for driving while intoxicated. "It happens to the best of us, Son," his dad said. "Please, don't let it happen again." Then dad hired a lawyer who got him off.

All his life, Justin has lived under a parental umbrella. His mother and father refused to allow him to grow up, and he never broke away. Because Justin never learned the meaning of the word *consequences*, he still thinks he can do anything he wants, whenever he wants, and somebody will be there to take care of him.

•

A person matures to the degree that (s)he and (s)he alone becomes responsible for the consequences of her/his decisions.

•

Life demands that we be individually responsible for our own decisions. Either we learn responsibility at home, or the world will teach us. When we don't learn at home, we get a more painful education from society, our peers, the police, or some other uncaring source.

### YOUR INTERNAL DIALOGUE

Back when you were developing your self-image, you were also working out an internal dialogue—that conversation you have in your head about what is going on with you and with the world outside. Powerful and controlling, this dialogue carries a distinct authority; it has the power to interpret and translate all the messages that come to you from the outside world. It supports and affirms your self-image.

•

Like two parts of a whole, your self-image and your internal dialogue work together in a symbiotic relationship.

•

Your internal dialogue constantly reinforces the way you see yourself. Good or bad, up-building or down-tearing, the dialogue that goes on in your head is the most authoritative voice you'll ever hear. Suppose someone were to say to you, "I really like you. I think you're one of the smartest, most clever people I've ever met." If your self-esteem supports that opinion of a smart, clever you, fine. Otherwise, your dialogue switches in and insists, "What's he up to? He wouldn't be complimenting and praising me unless he wanted something."

Human behavior is based on the inner dialogue going on inside a person's head.

•

Your inner dialogue controls your thinking
and your behavior.

•

Like your old self-image, your inner dialogue isn't even tied to you, or to who and what you are. It's tied to your parents as you were growing up, to childhood experiences, or to some other antiquated event.

## AFTER THE DECISION

Now that you have chosen to live in the future rather than in the past, you need to develop a new dialogue to support your decision. That new dialogue should reflect the reality of today. Are you:

- a successful businessperson?
- a conscientious parent?
- an honest person of integrity?
- a person of conscience?
- a person who takes good care of your physical self?

- an intellectually curious man or woman?
- a faithful volunteer for a worthwhile cause?

You have undoubtedly accomplished a lot, and you have a perfect right to think of yourself in terms of your successes. These things should be reflected in your new inner dialogue.

Start your new dialogue with your decision from the last chapter:

> *I am loved by God regardless of who else may or may not love me. I am okay even though everyone is not going to like me. Some will and some won't, but who I am is not based on that. My value and my place in this world do not turn on that hinge. I am okay as I am, who I am, where I am, here and now. This means I don't have to produce anything, impress anyone, live up to anything, or accomplish anything.*

You may say, "I can say the words, but they just don't seem true. The problem is, my husband (wife, children, boss, friend, relative) *makes me feel...."*

No, no! That's a lie you have been telling yourself.

•

Nobody makes you feel anything.

•

Your feelings are a *result* of what you say to yourself on the inside (your inner dialogue). Other people affect you and influence you, but the final authority for your feelings is *you* and *you alone.*

From this moment on, make a decision never to criticize yourself ever again. And refuse to accept criticism from anyone else. When someone else starts to criticize you, say, "Stop it. I do not take criticism. I take American Express, and I take Visa, but I do not take criticism. If you have advice, suggestions, or guidance, I will listen. But I am not willing to hear criticism of me."

Criticism is useless and negative. Your new dialogue is going to be:

- positive
- affirming
- complimentary
- encouraging.

If you are wondering what to say to yourself, a good start would be to complete the following statements:

I make myself happy by telling myself

_____

_____

_____

I depress myself by telling myself

_____

_____

_____

I excite myself by telling myself

_____

_____

_____

I encourage myself by telling myself

_____

_____

_____

Now add more positive statements about yourself. Learn to say them to yourself frequently.

## A NEW PARENT

You said good-bye to your position as a *child* of your mother and father. Although you will always be their son or daughter, you have given up the parent-child relationship for good. You have begun constructing a new self-image and a new internal dialogue for yourself. Yet you still have a huge emptiness inside you. What will fit into that hole?

You will!

You can parent yourself. *The feminine part of you will be your new mother* who will nurture, comfort, console, compliment, and care for that little child inside you. *The masculine part of you will be your new father* who will strengthen and encourage you, will set boundaries for you, and will make the factual decisions you need made.

•

As you become your own parents,
you finally become a truly autonomous person.

•

## PARENTING THE CHILD WITHIN YOU

Picture yourself as a three-year-old child. See your curly brown (straight black, long blond) hair and your little pug (freckled, sunburned) nose. See yourself in your little striped tee shirt and overalls (ruffled dress, shorts and shirt). How has the adult in you been treating that little child? If you grew up with criticism, you have probably been very critical of that little one inside you. If you were raised with impossibly high expectations, you have probably laid impossibly high expectations on that little child. If you were not taught limits and boundaries, you likely haven't set them for the child inside you.

"My parents had pretty rigid boundaries," says Janet. "Once they decided something, that was it. Not much was negotiable. As a result, there was little creativity and freedom in my family. When I reached adulthood, I was really driven in the area of responsibility. So what did I do? I married someone who had no boundaries. It was a classic case of opposites attracting.

"As soon as we married, I switched into my family's mode: I immediately started setting lots of boundaries for both of us. My husband wanted to relax and goof off, but I couldn't do it, and I couldn't allow him to. My inner dialogue parroted the phrases from my childhood:

- We are not going to spend good money on that! We can't afford it.
- Why can't you just stop and think before you do something?
- You have no business...!

"That strong 'work' ethic created a rigid parent inside of me who didn't cut much slack for the little girl inside to play, relax, and be creative. I couldn't do any of those things until I had done *all* the responsible things. So I'd 'steal time' by staying up all night to carve, sew, read, or do anything that I considered just pleasure. I was an adult in body, but my behavior was controlled by my childhood past."

•

We become the same type of parent to the child
inside us as our parents were to us.

•

This parent may be demanding, critical, encouraging, neglectful, unavailable, indulgent—you fill in the blank. Despite the futility and non-productivity, despite the hurt and pain, we seem locked into the cycle.

## BEING A GOOD PARENT

A good parent understands that the little child within—like all children—needs to be affirmed, reassured, and comforted. That's what your child needs from you. (S)he doesn't need to work constantly; there need to be times to play, to rest, to sleep. Treating the child within you in this positive way is your new dynamic.

Taking care of your inner child means you will do such things as:

- Set that little one down and say, "You are important enough for me to sit here and feed you. And not just feed you anything, but to feed you something nutritious."

That means you will put away the potato chips and candy bars and make yourself a salad. Then you will take time to sit at the table and eat. (And every now and then you will pull out a special treat, even if it isn't nutritious.)

- Say "no" when it is appropriate: "We won't eat that even though I know you love it." "We won't buy that however much you want it." "We won't go there even though I know you think it would be fun."

That means you will learn to say, "I have to say 'no' because I love you too much to let you do something that is not good for you."

- Say "yes" when there is no good reason not to: "I believe in you." "Go for it!" "I know you will be successful." "Have a wonderful time!" It means you will take every opportunity to encourage, affirm, and compliment the child within you. Make the decisions rather than allowing the little child to do so. The adult part of you is intelligent and trustworthy. You will hear the child's desires and wants. You will listen to them and consider them. But in the end, the adult part of you will make the decisions.

•

It means you don't put a child in charge.

•

- Refrain from parenting the child as a reenactment of history, according to the way your parents parented you. You may use some of the ideas and approaches they used, because the methods are still right today (such as encouraging principles, values, and morals). But what isn't right for you today, you will change or throw out.

It means keeping what is good and applicable today, and discarding what isn't.

## BEING A RESPONSIBLE PARENT

The temptation, now that you are in charge, will be to overcompensate for the hurts from your past. A woman might say, "I never had pretty things when I was a child. Now if I see something I like, I'm going to buy it. I won't even *look* at the price tag!" If she has unlimited funds, that may be fine. But most people don't. A more responsible reaction to the desire of that little girl within is to say, "Yes, honey, you can get this if it is really important to you. But you must remember, we will live within our means. So if we decide to get this, we can't get that." That's what we do with our children. We don't just hand them our credit cards.

Also, make sure the buying isn't an emotional compensation for some deeper need within you. In other words, don't throw things and dollars at your "child" when what the child really needs is to develop a creative outlet, a friendship, a hobby, a physical activity, or a comfortable home.

•

As a parent to your inner child, the aim of your initial decision is to be a nurturing, responsible, caring, loving, hearing, affirming parent to yourself.

•

Your assurance to that child is: "I'm going to talk to you differently. I'm going to treat you differently. I'm going to listen to what you have to say. And I will provide you with both permission and protection."

As a responsible parent, you can think and reason both for yourself and for your inner child. Begin by affirming:

- I can think.
- I do not expect anyone else to think for me.
- This is the way I am made; therefore, I will use my brain.
- I select what I think about and determine how long I dwell on various subjects.
- I can communicate with others and tell them what I need and want from them.

## TO HELP YOU PARENT WELL...

You can communicate with the little child within you. You know how to do that. But how will your inner child communicate with you? That child needs a language, and it will be a language of feelings. In many of our homes, feelings were not acceptable when we were growing up. So when we became adults, we ignored our feelings and gave them little value.

Sometimes the language of feelings is limited. Let's see what that language looks like set down on paper. We'll get you started, then you fill in as many feeling words as you can. (Remember, you are doing this exercise for your own little child. Don't try to do it perfectly. Just do it so that it *feels* right for you. Use your imagination. Allow yourself to be creative.)

happy

sad

glad

mad

upset

angry

peaceful

contented

Find at least 30 "feeling" words. That will provide a good vocabulary for your child to begin expressing him- or herself. But don't stop there. Continue to add to the list as more ideas come to you.

For the rest of today and tomorrow, and each day this week, go down this list every hour and pick out a feeling or two that you are experiencing. Your little child's strong emotional side operates 24 hours a day, 7 days a week, 365 days a year, whether you are awake or asleep. Your body is never idle, and your brain is always working. Your heart continues to beat, your blood pumps throughout your body, your lungs expand and contract. It's the same with your emotions. You are never emotionally idle either.

Once you become comfortable with this feeling vocabulary, at any given time you will be able to say to your little child, "Tell me what you're feeling now," and your child will be able to tell you. This keeps you in touch with yourself.

•

It produces an inner harmony.
It can be a new source of peace and contentment.

•

But *telling* is just half of communication. The other half is *listening*. It's very important that you listen to what your inner child feels, *because those feelings are the windows to your own needs*.

Do you see what you are doing here? You are building a new relationship with yourself. One that is based on reality. One that is contemporary and current. And one that can be communicated. This new relationship is not the one given to you by your parents; it is the one you choose. Here you can compensate for any hurts or pains you suffered as a child. Here you can literally build a new childhood for yourself.

## LEARNING BY REINFORCEMENT

It is difficult to break old patterns and make new ones. But it is possible. It takes time and patience and persistence, but it can be done. You will find that it's easier and you will be more successful if you constantly reinforce the new pattern.

Take some time right now to reinforce the new decision you made in the last chapter and repeated at the beginning of this one by saying it over five more times. (If you need to, look back at the beginning of this chapter. But if you have to peek, you'd better say it over ten more times.)

Now write out ten things you like about yourself. (Some examples might be: "I'm friendly," "I'm loyal," "I keep confidences," "I'm attractive," "I'm good with money," "I'm a generous person," "I'm dependable.")

If you find yourself balking at the idea of complimenting yourself, ask: *Why should complimenting myself be any less valid and legitimate than criticizing myself?* Actually, complimenting is healthier and more reasonable. You have permission to be extravagant with the compliments.

1. _____
2. _____
3. _____
4. _____
5. _____
6. _____
7. _____
8. _____
9. _____
10. _____

Do that every morning, five days a week, for four weeks.

*"But I can't even complete the first list of ten!"* some of you may be insisting.

Suppose you were asked to find ten things you could *criticize* about yourself. Could you do that? Probably so. Easily.

Since you are no longer going to say those critical things, turn them around and say positive things instead. For instance, if you are tempted to say, "I'm ugly!" remind yourself that that's a lie. You aren't ugly. That's just what you have learned to say about yourself. Say instead, "There are many attractive things about me. I have beautiful eyes. I am well-muscled...."

*"Okay. I'll start with: I have a pretty face even though I'm so heavy."*

Stop! Don't add that last part. State "I have a pretty face" and stop right there. Actually, don't stop there. Go on to add: "And I like my body. And I like my hands. And I like my hair. And I accept myself just the way I am right now. I'm a good friend. I'm loyal. I keep my word. I'm thoughtful, kind, decisive, and disciplined. I'm sensitive. I have a good sense of humor, and I'm a lot of fun."

If you insist that you *don't* like your body, ask yourself: "Am I not thankful I have a body? What if it were withered? Paralyzed? Hit by a truck? Destroyed by disease?

*"But I'm too heavy!"*

Too heavy compared to what?

•

All comparison is designed to make you
come out a loser.

•

Every time you compare, it is to discount yourself. You

say, "I'm fat compared to the models in magazines." You don't say, "I'm slender compared to the three-ton guy I read about in the *National Enquirer*."

You may not be satisfied with this or that about yourself. That's fine. Accept yourself as you are today, then set goals to change what it is you are not satisfied with.

The goal of this exercise is for you to do it long enough, and repeat the affirmations often enough, such that eventually they become a part of you. As you practice saying positive things to yourself, you will find that those positives replace the old negatives.

Your positive statements must overpower the negative voices from your past.

•

This is what we call building a new
internal dialogue.

•

## IT'S NEVER TOO LATE TO HAVE A
## HAPPY CHILDHOOD!

Since you are now responsible for yourself, get yourself pointed in an upward, outward direction. Tell yourself:

- My emotional state is my choice.
- All my feelings are God-given. They are neither good nor bad. The way I *express* them determines whether they are constructive or destructive.
- I choose my behavior and thoughts, and they produce my feelings.
- I will be aware of what I am telling myself in my head.
- I will be kind and gentle with myself.

Then focus on that good parenting. Listen to yourself saying: "I'm so tired! I'm absolutely exhausted because I've been working around the clock for three weeks. The company is upgrading the computer programs, designing equipment, and making all new forms for the plant workers. Everybody in the company has been working extremely long hours, and I'm totally exhausted."

When this happens, you are ignoring the basic needs of the little child inside you. You are not giving that child adequate rest. It's the same as if you had a three-year-old in your care who was pleading, "I'm so tired. Please, please let me sleep," and you were insisting, "No, you can't rest. We're going to keep working." Treat yourself with as much care and respect as you would treat a child. *You would never require a three-year-old to miss meals or a night's sleep. Take that same care, tenderness, thoughtfulness, and gentleness, and apply it to yourself.*

What if your job *requires* such pressure? Then you're in the wrong job! You are more important than your job, career, profession, or paycheck. It makes no difference who you are or how important your role. This is as true of the Chairmen of the Board and CEOs as of factory workers and garbage collectors. If you can't keep yourself healthy in the company where you work, resign. Working yourself to death isn't doing anyone a favor, not even the company.

•

Nothing is worth a heart attack.

•

Robert was the opposite of Justin, the young man we met at the beginning of this chapter. While Justin wouldn't take any responsibility, Robert took too much. He was in business with his father, and he never stopped working. He would literally run from his desk to the restroom, then back again. He always ate lunch at his desk. His car was the first in the parking lot in the morning, and he wouldn't leave at night until every other car was gone. At the age of 49, Robert was unmarried and had no social life at all. He was tense, nervous, and seriously depressed. Then one day his father dropped dead of a heart attack. His father's death caused Robert to take serious stock of his own life.

That was two years ago. Today, Robert manages the business. He no longer runs to and from the restroom. In fact, he makes a point of stopping to visit people on the way. His depression is gone, and his social life is... Well, let's just say he is engaged to be married.

Robert is taking care of the little child inside himself, and what a difference it's made. What's more, there is a new atmosphere in the office. And amazingly, production has increased steadily since Robert started changing.

So go for it! Have a happy childhood!

# 8
# TAKING CHARGE OF THE CHANGE

*"Iffen you like what you got,*
*keep on doin' what you're doin'.*
*But iffen you don't like what you got,*
*you better do somethin' else."*

Anthony, hard-living, hard-talking, hard-drinking, hard-working man of 58: "Come on! You mean I can change? *Me?* This crusty old chip off my old dad?"

Jean, small and slender, timid and fearful: "Me change? No, no, I don't think I could. I am who I am. This is who God made me to be."

Anthony and Jean misunderstand. It's not that we *can change*. It's that we *are changing*. Whether we want to or not. Whether we like it or not.

•

Change is the only constant in life.

•

"Nah," says Anthony. "I'm the same old Anthony I was when I was a kid. Except now I'm smarter about what I do. And now...."

Aha! Change.

"Well," Jean sighs, "I guess if it's for the good..."

Not only is change good, it is absolutely necessary. Where there is no change, there is no life. So instead of

95

"Can I really change?" the question is, "Who is in charge of my change?"

## WHO'S IN CHARGE?

Do you like who you are becoming? Are you satisfied with the person you are and the direction you are going?

"Well," Anthony concedes, "I've been married and divorced twice, and I have a girlfriend now, but I don't want to get married again if it's just going to be like before all over again."

"I always was a homebody," says Jean. "But now I don't want to leave even to visit my son 20 miles away. I like my home, but it's almost like I'm becoming a prisoner here."

It is time for Anthony and Jean to take charge of their lives.

•

Unless you take control of the change
that is inevitably taking place,
the change will control your destiny.

•

The time to take charge is now.

## MAKING YOUR CHANGES

You have made the decision to start taking care of yourself in a new and different way. You have determined that you will affirm yourself, and that you will set appropriate boundaries. You are listening to the little child within you and learning what that little one needs. You understand that you are totally responsible for your own happiness and contentment in life. And you realize that unless you make these changes, there is nobody but yourself to hold accountable.

Now, it's time to begin making specific changes that will take what you know in your head and put it into action in your life. These changes can be

- emotional
- physical
- social
- financial
- mental
- spiritual.

Or they can be of any other type.

Write out a list of at least 20 changes you are willing to make.

The changes must be visible, specific, and measurable so that you will know for sure when you made each one.

1. _____
   _____

2. _____
   _____

3. _____
   _____

4. _____
   _____

5. _____
   _____

6. _____
_____
_____

7. _____
_____
_____

8. _____
_____
_____

9. _____
_____
_____

10. _____
_____
_____

11. _____
_____
_____

12. _____
_____
_____

13. _____
_____
_____

14. _____
_____
_____

15. _____
_____
_____

16. _____
_____
_____

17. _____
_____
_____

18. _____

_____

_____

19. _____

_____

_____

20. _____

_____

_____

If you were not able to think of 20, keep thinking and fill them in as they come to you. If you did fill in all 20, you might want to get another piece of paper and record more.

## AIM FOR THE *SPECIFIC* AND THE *DEFINITIVE*

Look back at what you wrote. Were you *specific* and *concrete* in what you listed? For instance,

"*I will change the way I dress*"

is a commendable change, but it is rather general. How will you actually proceed? You might add,

"*On Saturday I will buy two new ties and one new dress shirt.*"

If you wrote,

"*I'm going to take better care of my belongings,*"

you might add,

"*Every Saturday I will get my car washed, and I will have*

*the oil changed every 5,000 miles."*

Specifics help get you focused.
One man stated:

*"I'm going to do a better job of interacting with the people who work with me."*

Pushed for specifics, he added:

*"I'm going to learn the names of the spouses and children of each of the people who work closely with me."*

Later he came in to report the difference his change had made. He said, "I went into the office and said 'hello' to my secretary as usual, and, as usual, she mumbled 'hello' back without missing a keystroke on her computer. Then I said, 'How is your husband, Will? I haven't seen him since the Christmas dinner.' My secretary stopped typing in mid-sentence. Puzzled, she looked up at me and said, 'Well, he's had a bad case of the flu, but he's much better now. Thank you for asking.' She seemed so genuinely pleased that I continued, 'Say, isn't Stacy in high school now?' She promptly pulled out her daughter's class picture to show me. We didn't talk more than two minutes, but since then, I've noticed that the entire atmosphere of our office has changed."

The man did not change his secretary. He changed himself. As a result of taking specific action on his three-line resolution, he transformed his working environment.

If you implement the decisions you wrote down, what difference will it make in your life and in the life of your family? What will you gain? If you don't implement the decisions you wrote down, what will you lose?

## CHANGE THE ROUTINE

It may be that not all the things you wrote down were bad things. In some cases, you may have merely wanted a change.

That's great. You need not limit your list to harmful routines. Think in terms of making changes in your routine... *period*.

- Try doing something different on Saturdays.
- Buy a totally different piece of clothing.
- Change your hairstyle.
- Change your makeup.
- Drive a different route to work.
- Go to bed and get up at a different time.
- Talk to people you don't usually talk to.
- Write letters to people you have never written to before.
- Give a gift to someone who has never given one to you.
- If you always eat in the kitchen, eat at the dining room table—maybe even use the fancy linen tablecloth and the good china!
- Offer to do the dinner dishes.
- Give the children a bath and read them a bedtime story.
- Sing out loud.
- Plant a few herbs outside your kitchen door and use them in your cooking.

While these things are not significant in themselves, they can help contribute to an overall feeling of getting out of the old rut. That will help change your perspective on life. It will help you to see the trees, or the new office buildings, on your way to work instead of that same old stripe in the road. You will find yourself staying more in the present because you don't know where every single house, bush, and stop sign is. Also, everything you do differently supports you and your new position of change.

While you're at it, why not get yourself a new look? You may look great the way you are. On the other hand, you may not be making the most of what God has given you. Either way, try some changes in your clothes, the way you wear your hair, your makeup. Make it a priority to start looking the nicest for the people who mean the most to you (hopefully, that's your family!).

Make some big changes, too, ones that can affect your future.

- Find out about your finances and investments. Study them. Claim them as your own. Know where you stand on insurance—life, health, fire, liability, and so forth.

- Get a good grasp on your income tax return. Never, ever sign a joint return—or any other document, for that matter—without understanding just what you are signing. If that means paying for some time with an accountant or lawyer, do it. It's well worth the investment.

- Pay attention to what you read. Choose things that bring joy and happiness into your life. Put away the books and articles that leave you sad, anxious, or afraid. Be careful what you watch on television and which movies you see. Choose things that lift you up rather than bring you down.

- Read something that stretches your brain, something not related to your work. Your brain needs exercise just like your body does. Read a book about polar bears or Marco Polo or the history of photography. Learning is good for you. It not only expands your brain, but it makes you a more interesting person.

- Build an emotional support system. Find a couple of friends with whom you can talk about what you've learned, where you are in life, what you are experiencing, where you have succeeded and where you have been defeated. Talk about where you're going with your life and what your challenges are. That way you will have a built-in support system, and also a couple of people to whom you'll be accountable. And when you have a real win, you'll have someone ready to celebrate with you.

- Just as you likely have a good physical support system— a doctor and a dentist for instance—also build up an emotional support system. Start with three good friends and your minister, priest, or rabbi. You may want to add a few other people, and perhaps a counselor as well.

## NO MORE CRITICISM—EVER!

Add this mantra to your self-dialogue (another good thing to tape to your bathroom mirror, by the way):

•

I will never criticize myself at any time for any reason. I will never accept criticism from anyone at any time for any reason. I will never criticize another person at any time for any reason.

•

Although few of us enjoy being criticized, too many of us invite it. We say such things as:

- *"This suit makes me look old."*
- *"This dress makes me look fat, doesn't it?"*
- *"I am so tired! Do I look as bad as I feel?"*
- *"Nobody appreciates me."*
- *"I'm sorry about this spaghetti. I guess I'm not a very good cook."*
- *"Oh, my hair! I've been fighting with it all day!"*
- *"I don't have that report done. I should have spent more time on it."*
- *"This probably sounds crazy, but....*

We are much more conditioned to give and receive criticism than to give and receive compliments. Begin to change that by *giving compliments and praise to yourself internally*. It will help the attitude you display to others. Invite praise by praising others. And be ready to receive praise without diminishing it. When someone offers you a compliment, instead of responding with, "Oh, that was nothing. Actually, I just...." try: "Thank you *so* much! I really appreciate your saying so." When you accept a compliment graciously, you make that other person feel good, too.

Virginia, a colleague of ours, recalls an evening after she had given a presentation. As she was walking to her car, a lady came up behind her and said, "Isn't that an absolutely beautiful...."

Since Virginia was already watching the sun sinking low in a gorgeous pink, crimson, and golden sky, she fully expected the lady to say "...sunset!" Instead she said, "...color on you!"

Caught completely off guard, Virginia stammered, "How nice of you to say that! It totally surprised me. I thought you were going to say 'what a beautiful sunset.'"

Thank you for such a sweet compliment."

The lady smiled broadly and said, "And your hair is so beautiful, too."

"Well, thank you," Virginia responded. "I think I got it from my grandmother. She had hair this color." Then, noticing the lady's thick, chestnut hair, Virginia added, "You have beautiful hair, too."

Suddenly the lady's demeanor changed. "Oh, I just wish my hair was one color!"she said self-consciously. "It's that mixed sort of nothing color."

Make the most of compliments that come your way. They will help you reinforce and internalize positive images of yourself.

## A COMPLIMENTARY ASSIGNMENT

Here is an assignment for you:

• Compliment yourself at least three times a day.

•

Tell yourself:

- "I've done a good job with this report."
- "That was a difficult situation and I really handled it well."
- "I swam 20 laps today. I'm really getting in shape."
- "I wanted cookies, but I ate carrots. Good for me!"

The more you practice complimenting yourself, the more natural and comfortable it will feel. And the more you will internalize those compliments. *The time will come when you will automatically think of yourself in positive terms.* And there will be a bonus: You will find a new ability to compliment and praise other people, a trait that will enrich and enhance your social life.

## BUT WHAT IF...?

"What if I need to gently criticize another person to help that person change?"

Don't do it! *There is only one person on earth you can change, and that is you.* If you expect others to change because you want them to, you are setting yourself up for disappointment and resentment. If that person changes, it will be because he or she wants to, not because of your criticism, however "gentle" or well intentioned. If that person asks your opinion, fine. If not, keep it to yourself.

"But what if someone criticizes me?"

There are several ways you can deflect criticism. You can:

• **Change the subject. Example:**

**Person:** *"If you keep eating like that, you're going to get fat."*

**You:** *"I love having lunch outside like this. When we finish, let's take a walk around the block."*

• **Handle it with humor. Example:**

**Person:** *"I can't believe you wore that!"*

**You:** *"Well, believe it! Because here I am, and I like what I'm wearing."*

### • Ask a direct question. Example:

**Person:** *"You're not doing that right. You need to sand it more. And that color won't look good.*
**You:** *"Are you criticizing my work?"*

### • Turn it into a compliment. Example:

**Person:** *"Is that the new dress you got?"*
**You:** *"Yes it is, and thank you for noticing. I really like it!"*

Sometimes, no matter what you say or do, a person will continue to criticize you. If that's the case, you might want to kindly tell him or her how you feel:

"You know, I have made a decision not to criticize anyone and not to allow anyone to criticize me. When you say things like that, I feel bad. Please don't do it."

If it continues, do what you can to avoid being around that person. If it's the person you're married to, go get some counseling. You're going to need it!

If the critical person is your parent, it's going to be harder.

Parents sometimes think it is their responsibility to criticize and correct. Start out with a gentle tactic, such as changing the conversation.

**Mother:** *"Your hair is getting awfully long and stringy. It never looked good long."*
**You:** *"Thanks for making me a cup of hot chocolate this morning, Mom. You know just how I like it."*

If she just doesn't get it and the criticism continues, perhaps you can sit down and talk to her.

**Mother:** *"I was talking about your hair. Why don't you cut it?"*

**You:** *"I don't think you intend this the way I'm perceiving it, Mom, but all this talk about my hair seems like criticism. I just wonder if you're aware of that and what we can do about it, because it doesn't feel good. I know you love me, and I know you wouldn't want to hurt me."*

If she still persists, be more definite.

**Mother:** *"I'm just telling you for your own good. I'd think you'd want to look your nicest."*

**You:** *"Don't tell me, Mom. Please, do not tell me. If you want to be with me, you must stop criticizing me."*

One warning: be sure that you are not inviting the criticism by failing to *keep the authority and the responsibility in the same spot.* For instance, you can't decide to take money from your parent, and then refuse to take the advice that comes along with it. Here's an example of what we mean:

**You:** *"Mom, my hair is driving me crazy but I can't afford to have it done. Could you pay for me to have a perm?"*

**Mother:** *"Again? Why don't you just get it cut? You spend so much time and money trying to get it to do what it just isn't going to do."*

**You:** *"Oh, great! Here you go again about my hair!"*

The exception to not accepting criticism is from a person of an advanced age. Some people do not grow old gracefully. They lose their perspective of reality and relationships. If this is true of your parent, be as kind and patient as you can. Let the comments go past you, and concentrate on affirming yourself. Remember, you may be there yourself one day.

## DIFFERENT RESPONSES

Some people may not respond positively to your changes. After all, those people knew the old you. They were familiar with the way you've always done things. Even though they might not like some of those patterns, still they have established relationships with you based on how you've always been. Now here you are making changes. Some people will be delighted, but others may ask:

- *"What's the matter with you? You aren't being yourself."*
- *"You're not like you've always been. What happened?"*
- *"I don't like this new you."*
- *"You're not the person I married.*

Eliza had been depressed all her life. After her husband died of a heart attack at the age of 38, she plunged into a depression so deep that it completely immobilized her. She spent all her time in bed with the door closed and the shades drawn. Her young children took care of themselves the best they could, but finally they had to ask the neighbors for help. The woman was taken to the hospital, and when she got out, she came to see us.

It took time, but the change in her was dramatic. She

began to function like she never had before. She got up in the morning and got the older children off to school, she bought groceries and cooked, she even smiled and hummed as she worked around the house.

One day while the older children were at school, she was in the yard watching her seven-year-old son play with their new kitten. At the sight of the two of them tumbling around after each other, the woman began to laugh out loud. The little boy froze. Then he ran over and threw himself on his mother and pounded her with his little fists.

"Stop it! Stop it!"he cried. "You're not my mother! My mother doesn't laugh!"

When you change, even when it is clearly for the better, the people around you may see it as a threat. It can upset the interaction between you.

It may help for you to explain the new behavior in yourself. If your spouse says, "You're not the person I married!"an appropriate response would be, "Hurrah! I'm changing and I'm growing."

Should your mother say, "It used to be so easy to get along with you. Now, I just can't understand you," you might answer, "Mother, I've been working on myself and I'm making some changes. You'll find me responding to you in different ways than in the past. But I want you to know that I still love you just as much, and that I will not under any circumstances be disrespectful to you."

Your spouse may be suspicious or uncooperative or unresponsive once you are no longer your comfortable, old, depressed, withdrawn, or angry self. She may decide, "He says he's changed, but he doesn't mean it. It's all an act," or "This isn't going to last," or "Here he is, trying to manipulate me again," or simply, "What is going on here?!

•

Change will require constancy, concentration, and strength from you.

•

It's your responsibility to hold tight to your change patterns. When the other people get used to the new you, they will become comfortable with you again. If some of your old friends never can accept the changes, then maybe they were not healthy relationships in the first place. Perhaps you would be better off making new friends. Certainly, *you* will be a happier, healthier person. A woman we'll call Sandy and her husband had a big fight, and she had stormed out of the house, vowing never to return. Six months had passed, and she was living with her parents. After taking control and making changes in her life, she packed everything she had at her parents' house and went back to the house where her husband was still living. "I'm moving back in," she announced to her astonished husband. "We're husband and wife, and we're going to make this marriage work." She proceeded to tell him, "I've behaved like a spoiled brat and I'm sorry. I really do apologize. I want you to know I have made some changes in myself, and I'm not going to behave like that any more. You have a new wife."

Her husband thought, *"Yeah, right!"*

But before long, he had to admit that Sandy really had changed. "She's a different woman," he said, "I love her like I never did before."

About two months later he called and said, "My wife is so happy! If I come over there, can you do the same thing to me that you did to her?" That was ten years ago. Sandy and her husband are still happily married, and they are now the parents of a daughter and twin baby boys.

It was Sandy's determination and consistency that made the difference.

Not only may the changes feel wrong to those around you, they may even feel wrong to you. You are out of your pattern, after all. The changes may even feel sinful. A standard response is, *"What you are teaching me is pure selfishness!"*

If by selfish you mean taking appropriate care of your-self, then, yes, that is what we're saying.

•

Until you possess a self,
you can't be loving toward another.

•

Rather than being self-*ish*, too many people are self-*less*.

Before you can love someone else, you have to first love yourself.

Before you can accept someone else, you have to first accept yourself.

Before you can forgive someone else, you have to first forgive yourself.

## TAKE PLEASURE IN GROWTH

What do you do for fun at home by yourself?

So many of us have become accustomed to being entertained by the television or by going out that we don't know how to actively play. We have developed a way to be happy and content in our own company. Not that there's anything wrong with watching some television or going out. (Some people, however, do decide to turn off the TV for one month.) But good emotional health calls for learn-ing how to entertain ourselves, by ourselves, in our own homes. This could be:

- gardening
- painting
- building model trains
- furniture building
- basket weaving
- needlepoint
- Chinese cooking
- bird watching
- calligraphy
- meditation
- prayer
- reading a classic

- restoring a classic car
- stenciling the walls
- listening to classical music
- keeping a journal

Or it could be any one of countless other activities. The thing is, it should be something that is truly fun for you. Something you can take pride in. Something where you say, "I can't wait until I can get home and...!"It's playtime for that little child inside you.

Get some ideas for "playtime" by:

- asking friends what they do.

- looking over the adult education courses offered in your area.

- visiting craft centers and places that offer cooking classes.

- watching the newspaper to see who is offering what— recreation centers, hobby stores, community centers. When something catches your eye as a possibility, sign up for it and give it a try. A class might give you just the jump-start you need.

It doesn't have to be a craft type hobby, of course. Maybe there is a sport you've always wanted to get involved in or a musical instrument you want to learn to play. Do it and have fun.

Don't overlook community volunteer work. It can be a wonderfully healthy outlet. Helping a child learn to read or seeing the welcoming smile of someone who seldom sees a visitor can restore your soul. And to the people who benefit—those in nursing homes, hospitals, and schools, or the homeless or disabled—you can be a veritable breath of life in an otherwise sad and dreary world. Volunteering can bring a dimension of meaning to life you have never known before.

Whatever activity you choose, the little child inside you will delight in this new activity, *"Just for me!"*

# 9
## SINK—OR RELATE

*"I finally discovered she was asking me to
carry baggage I didn't pack.
And it didn't even have my name on it!"*

Joanne doesn't cook or clean. "That's not my thing," she explains. "Never was." Her husband, Ken, earns a good salary, and she is able to be a stay-at-home mom for their third and fifth grade children. After a breakfast of whatever can be stuck into the toaster, she drives the kids to school, then heads for the gym where she works out for an hour and a half. Two days a week she has tennis lessons, and on Fridays she plays with a group of friends. She has charity meetings to attend, friends to lunch with, a book club to prepare for, soccer games and ballet lessons to drive to.

"By the end of the day, I'm exhausted," she says. "But what does Ken do when he gets home from work? Nothing! He doesn't help with the kids or anything. I'm lucky if I can get him to pick something up for dinner."

Joanne was devastated when she discovered that her Ken was having an affair with his secretary.

Sometimes it seems to Beverly that all she *does* is cook and clean. After she gets home from her job as a teacher's aide, that is. Allan, Beverly's husband of 35 years, doesn't work. He got tired of the old grind and took advantage of his company's offer of an early retirement. The money really isn't enough to live on, so Beverly needs to keep working for another seven to ten years. Allen stays busy with his hobbies—gardening and building model trains— but he doesn't do any of the housework. He says he's worked all his life and he has earned his rest.

"He's never done any work at home, not even running to the grocery store," Beverly says with resignation. "To him, it's all women's work." So she continues to do it all.

In one way or another, we all relate to other people. We need to. Humans are made for social interaction in a way that goes beyond basic survival. We interact and relate in order to establish who we are, to find out who they are, and to discover our relationship toward each other. We do not really know who we really are until we see our reflection in the eyes of another person. We do not know we are heard and understood until we hear another's response to what we say. We mirror each other's existence.

The essential nature of human life makes us seek and cultivate relationships. My decision to relate is a decision to live at the level of a human being. If I choose instead to use (and abuse) people, I relate at a level that is less than human.

•

Relating is living.

•

## THE HEALTH OF YOUR RELATIONSHIPS

*"A relationship? Well, what's in it for me?"*
*"Friends? That depends. How can they benefit me?"*
People seldom say it in so many words, but unfortunately it's not uncommon to approach relationships selfishly. A selfish approach demands:

- You are responsible for always making me happy.

- You shall never put any interests above me.

- You must know what I want and feel without my having to tell you.

- Whenever I do something for you, you must do something just as good—or better—for me.

- You must protect me from anxiety, worry, hurt, and pain.

- I expect to get my sense of self-worth and esteem from you.

- You will be grateful for everything I do for you, and never disapprove.

- You will be so caring and loving that I'll never need to make myself vulnerable in any way.

Taking this approach to relationships will put you directly into one of the three positions set down by Steve Karpman:

**VICTIM** = **Always blames others for everything that happens.**

**RESCUER** = **Always out to "help" and "fix" everyone else instead of taking care of him or herself.**

**PERSECUTOR** = **Criticizes and passes judgment on everyone.**

Karpman demonstrates this killer cycle of relationships in his "Karpman Triangle":

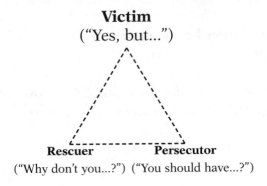

**Victim**
("Yes, but...")

**Rescuer**                **Persecutor**
("Why don't you...?")  ("You should have...?")

All three are loser positions. Nobody wins. And all three are destructive in a relationship.

**Victims** are the ones who refuse to look after and take care of themselves. They are always out of luck, out of money, out of friends, out of time, out of gas. Meet a victim, and he will tell you about all the people who have let him down. He's suffered a lot, but it's always someone else's fault. And he inevitably seems helpless to do anything about it.

**Rescuers** are victims' best friends. Victims couldn't keep going without them. They are always searching for someone to help. They get flowers for the sick, cookies for the neighbors, bandages for skinned knees, and Hints from Heloise for anyone who will listen. If they can find somebody in need, they are thrilled. Needless to say, they are always exhausted. They are so worn out from fixing everyone else that they never have time to take care of themselves. And everyone else is indebted to them. They always ignore one specific person, however—themselves.

(Sometimes rescuers go so far as to marry victims!)

**Persecutors** are quick to make judgments—on everybody! To them, everyone fits snugly into a specific category. You can hear one coming a mile off:

- *"It's those danged Republicans!"*
- *"It's those crazy Democrats!"*
- *"Women drivers!"*
- *"Men are slobs!"*

They are convinced that if only everyone would listen to them, this world would be a better place. Don't share a problem with a persecutor. That person will have a ready answer: "Well, you should have...."

We all get caught up in these unhealthy positions. We move among them. If one isn't working, we simply go on to another. (Can you see how Joanne and Ken, and Beverly and Allan, fit into the triangle and how they move from one position to another?) The goal is to gain control over someone else rather than adequately taking care of yourself.

Some people are staunchly devoted to one specific category. A good "card-carrying" **rescuer**, for instance, can make a victim of almost anyone. Watch this:

*"Randy, what's the matter?"*
*"Nothing. I'm fine."*
*"You don't look fine."*
*"No, no. I'm okay. Maybe just a little tired."*
*"Now, Randy, I've known you for a long time. If anyone knows when there's something wrong with you, it's me. And I'm telling you, there's something wrong."*
*"Well...maybe I will take a little rest."*
*"Okay, and please, please call if there's something I can do.*

*Better yet, I'll give you a call later on today. Maybe then you can tell me what's really bothering you."*
Randy started out fine, and now look at him!

There are also black-belt **victims**. A really good one can work ten rescuers to death.

*"What's the matter, Bob?"*
*(sigh) "Nothing."*
*"Oh, please, tell me."*
*"Do you really want to know?" (pause) "Do you really care?"*
*"Yes I do. Maybe I can help."*
*"Well, I got fired from my job this morning. Me, the hardest worker in the place! Everyone there had it in for me. A whole bunch of them got together and started talking about me and accusing me of everything under the sun. There was no truth in any of it."*
*"That's so sad!"*
*"Well, you'd think I'd be used to it by now. The same thing happened to me in my last job, and the job before that. I don't know why it always has to be me."*
*"Did you talk to your supervisor?"*
*"It wouldn't do any good. You know how supervisors are."*
*"You know, Bob, I know someone in that company. I could call her and see if she might be able to do something."*
*"Oh, no, don't do that. I'm so upset I wouldn't work there now if it was the last place on Earth."*
*"Well, I do have a friend who is looking to hire someone. Maybe I could get you on there."*
*"Oh, well, I'm afraid after all that's happened to me, I'm going to need a little time to recuperate."*
Roy can give Bob 99 suggestions, and not one will work for him. He is committed to this victim position, and he is going to go through life waiting for people to come

along and fix things for him.

Now watch an experienced **persecutor** at work:

*"I need to tell you something. It may hurt, but it's for your own good. I'm the only one who cares enough to be really honest with you. The thing is, nobody really likes you. Everyone's just kind to you out of pity. You have no friends. I just thought you needed to know."*
Or:
*"The trouble with this country is all those (enter category of your choice). They are the ones that cause all the trouble. They have no business here. We're the ones who pay the taxes and support the government. I think 'they' ought to take everyone of them and...."*

*Refuse to be in any of these positions!* If your goal is to have a relationship, please understand that victim—rescuer—persecutor is a sinking cycle. Pull yourself out, and don't let anyone suck you back in.

How? Refuse to participate. To a victim you might say, *"I'm sorry about what happened at work. Let me know if there is something you want me to do."* To a rescuer, *"There really is nothing wrong,"* then change the subject. To a persecutor, *"You know, this isn't getting us anywhere. I'm sorry if I upset you. Let's just drop it."*

The end.

If the other person responds:

*"There really is something wrong with you!"* or
*"You don't really care!"* or
*"DON'T YOU WALK AWAY FROM ME!"*

you can simply busy yourself with something else, in another area if possible. Do not allow him or her to pull you back in.

Take care of yourself. Don't expect anyone else to do it for you.

•

Do not do for other people what they can do for themselves. And don't allow anyone else to do for you what you are capable of doing for yourself.

•

We have a cardinal rule about communication: *Don't talk unless the other person is listening.* Talk is only helpful if someone else is hearing what is said. You can tell when that other person stops hearing. If you keep on talking, you're going to end up feeling like a victim, or you're going to start persecuting someone else.

•

When the listening stops, stop talking.

•

You have learned to love (and forgive) yourself, and you're ready to start loving (and forgiving) another human being. It doesn't matter whether or not she likes you right now. However unhappy she is, you don't have to defend yourself. Instead, choose to remind yourself:

*"Right now, she isn't happy with me. But I still love me and God loves me. If I made a mistake, I'll apologize. But I will not put any other person in charge of me."*

## THE LESSON OF THE HULA HOOPS

A person's inner world is his or her own personal kingdom where that person puts himself totally in charge. Inside our inner world is everything that makes us who we are: thoughts, feelings, past, present, future, dreams, failures, successes—everything. Inside this world the person can decide:

> *"I'm okay, because God loves me. Therefore, because God loves me, I have decided to love myself and to love God in return. This means I'm okay with who I am here and now. This does not mean I have reached perfection. It simply means my worth and value are now based on who I am to God—accepted, loved, and forgiven. I understand that my daily mistakes and failures do not change this fact."*

This becomes the reference point for that person's worth and value.

Let's see how this works: Here are two people, a married couple we'll call Scott and Julie. Their hula hoops represent their individual inner worlds.

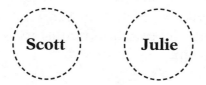

Scott and Julie have complete control and authority over everything inside their respective hula hoops, but zero authority over anything outside it. They can have influence—an effect—on the outside world, but they cannot control it. At the same time, Scott has no control over Julie's inner world within her hula hoop, and Julie has no control over Scott's. They can affect and influence each other's internal world, but they have no authority over it. Scott's personal worth is not based on his relationship with Julie, nor is Julie's based on her relationship with Scott. This doesn't mean Scott is always right. It just means he no longer has to prove anything, achieve anything, perform, convince, or answer to anyone else for who he is. The same is true with Julie.

This healthy space inside their own hula hoops is what Scott and Julie require in order to form a healthy relationship with each other—or with anyone else, for that matter. If they do not do this, they will go into every relationship from a position of neediness, doing their best to get from another person what they should be giving themselves:

- security
- worth
- identity
- value
- self-esteem

## A RELATIONSHIP BOND

Now, let's look at a picture of Scott and Julie after they are in a marriage (courtship, friendship, business, or any other) relationship:

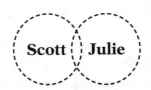

The overlapped part of the two hula hoops is the part we call *the relationship*. Since Scott brings a loved person to the relationship, he doesn't come to get loved. He brings a whole person, complete and secure. Julie does the same.

•

The measure of the value of their relationship is the overlap of his loved life with her loved life.

•

This overlap enriches and enhances his life, and it does not diminish her. The same is true with the loved life Julie brings in. Neither Scott nor Julie is depleted by the relationship. On the contrary, both are better, richer, happier, and more complete because of the relationship.

In a healthy relationship, neither person is saying, "Oh my goodness, I don't know how much longer I can stand this together stuff!" That's because there is an area of privacy in their lives where their hula hoops do not overlap. This private, secure area where *God loves me, I love me, and I love God* is the wellspring that continually enriches and enhances the part that is characterized by mutuality. It is the private, internal area where each is always loved, accepted, and forgiven even on those days when they don't feel love, acceptance, and forgiveness for each other.

## THE SIZE OF THE OVERLAP

Sometimes the overlap between two people is to the ultimate, sometimes it's moderate, sometimes it's non-existent. Marriage is designed to overlap to the max. Yet even a marriage isn't static. It doesn't stay at that point. There are times when there is a great deal of overlap, and when two people share a whole lot of their lives and thoughts and feelings, it's very intensive and intimate. But there are other times when they are apart. They may be having a difficult time in the relationship, and they may have withdrawn some from that overlapped space.

Other relationships are designed for very slight overlaps. A casual friendship is an example, the relationship you develop with a business co-worker with whom you do a project. You may talk a little bit about your families, but you don't tell each other much about your feelings or your philosophy of life or how you vote. Only a little bit of your inner worlds overlap.

•

Even in the closest and most intimate of
relationships, both people are,
and must remain, autonomous.

•

Each person is in charge of his or her own life. Both are enriched and enhanced, and neither is diminished. Together, they become more than just two solitary people. Theirs is a position in which 1 + 1 = 3. Their common, shared life makes their individual lives richer and fuller than they could ever be alone.

## CLAIM YOUR SPACE

Claiming your space will give you a security, safety, comfort, integrity and strength that will enable you to love even when the other person is acting unlovable.

Is your relationship so intimate that you can't live without each other? Then run to the nearest exit! If you find a person you can't live without, you are going to become dependent on that person and neither of you will be happy. In the end, that person is going to resent you, or you are going to resent that person.

•

Dependency always breeds resentment.

•

Here is what we mean:

**Mark Debbie**

This is a good picture of what a healthy relationship is *not*. These two people, Mark and Debbie, have everything in common: matching tee-shirts, matching pajamas, color-coordinated outfits when they go out. And they *do* everything together. Mark wants Debbie to be his shadow, and Debbie wants Mark to be her shadow. They can even finish one another's sentences. At first Debbie loves it; Mark takes care of the money and does all the other things she hates doing. But somewhere down the line, it begins to feel an awful lot like control, and she doesn't like it any more. She even chafes when he explains, "I'm just trying to take care of you!"With no private lives of their own, Debbie has to keep Mark happy, and Mark has to keep Debbie happy. Either they are both happy together, or they are both unhappy. Heaven forbid that one be happy without the other!

Without space, it is impossible to maintain a marriage for any length of time. It's easy to love a person who is being lovable, but human beings are not always lovable. For a couple to be committed for a lifetime, the task is to love one another when the other is being unlovable. The goal in a healthy relationship is for each person to be able to come on a regular basis as a loving person to the relationship, and to willingly give the other person time to get to a different place in his world.

•

A healthy relationship means refusing to keep score or maintain a failure file on each other.

•

It means being willing to forgive
over
and over
and over again.

Because none of us is perfect, if we stop forgiving it's just a matter of time before the relationship is over.

On the other hand, forgiveness does not require that we continue in the relationship. Sometimes relationships just do not work, and they need to end. When that happens, the important thing is to end it from a position of forgiveness.

## TAKE RESPONSIBILITY, GIVE RESPONSIBLITY

If you will say:

- I will give to you the same responsibility I assume for myself.

- I will not take over your responsibility or ask you to take over mine.

- I am responsible for my behavior and feelings. You are responsible for yours. That way we can each be a complete person.

- When you are temporarily incapacitated, I will

freely help you.

- When I am temporarily incapacitated, you will freely help me.

- I can move toward you as a complete being.

- I can accept you as a whole person.

- I will love only God with all my heart, soul, mind, and strength—not any person, including you.

Then you have the right to state:

- I will love you as I love myself.

Of course, you cannot be in a relationship and then forge ahead saying any old thing you want to and acting any old way at any old time. That's not being responsible. It certainly isn't being empathetic and sensitive to the other person. There are rules that must not be ignored.

A strong, growing relationship is one in which each of you is accepting responsibility, and then willingly giving it. At the same time, each person is sensitive and doing his or her best to meet the needs of the other person.

## MAKE YOURSELF A PERSON...

We tend to focus on what other people should do in order to have a good relationship with us. We spend a lot of time and energy hoping they will, trying to get them to, wondering why they don't, and wishing they would. How much more beneficial it would be for us to focus on the person we bring *into* the relationship!

We all have friends we can hardly wait to be with. If we

are to be people worth relating to, we would do well to ask ourselves what it is that attracts us to others, then see if we have those traits in our own lives.

### A strong, healthy relationship is built
### by a person who is:

- affirming
- courteous
- kind
- polite
- non-judgmental
- warm
- loving
- accepting
- compassionate
- willing to share my interests
- interested in me personally
- strong
- pro-active rather than passive
- able to share at an honest level
- positive about life
- fun to be with
- continually has fun things going in life
- living an interesting life
- growing rather than remaining static
- willing to listen
- living a life in process and is growing and changing
- bringing diversity to life by sharing new things
- stretching my imagination or creativity

### Strong, healthy relationships are not built
### by a person who is:

- needy
- sarcastic
- dependent
- enabling
- compliant
- into one-upsmanship
- insistent on being better, smarter, more talented, or stronger
- competitive

- accepting of my
  unattractive, damaging
  behavior
- ready to spread gossip

- critical
- pessimistic
- cynical

Go back over these two lists and put a check beside the words and phrases that apply to you.

How many were you able to check off in the first list? That gives you an idea of how close you are to being the kind of a person other people would want to have in a relationship.

Did you have to check off some in the second list? That shows you where you need work.

•

When you make changes for yourself,
with yourself, and by yourself,
the strength and security you gain is contagious.

•

When you change, watch those around you catch what you have!

As Happy As You Want To Be!

# 10
# WE HAVE MET THE ENEMY

*"Do you have a travel agent for your guilt trips?"*

Did you know you have a family of dragons in your basement? You do! We all do. They are the fears and anxieties we bring from childhood into our adult lives—old memories or experiences painful to remember. The constant recalling of these feelings or experiences turns them into monsters in our minds. The more we recall them, the larger and stronger they grow.

The powerful old patriarchs and matriarchs hold sway over their dragon children, their children's children, and more dragon nieces and nephews than you can count.

Those dragons lurking in the shadows are no pets. They prevent you from having the type of relationships you desire and the quality of life that can lead you to true personal fulfillment. They give you your dark thoughts and disturb your sleep, and they prevent you from having a rich, full, free, and happy life.

## GRANDFATHER DRAGON FEAR
## AND
## GRANDMOTHER DRAGON GUILT

Talk about fearful monsters! These are two of the worst. They are huge and threatening, powerful with experience.

## Grandfather Dragon Fear

Fear, the granddaddy of all dragons, is basic to most of the problems we have in life. Back when our ancestors lived in caves, fear protected them. It kept humans alert and watchful, and therefore alive. As we became more civilized, we developed other kinds of protective fear:

- fear that protected our families
- fear that protected our pride
- fear that protected our position
- fear that protected our reputations.

For the most part, these, too, are healthy, functional fears. They help us set limits and boundaries on where we go and what we do.

But somewhere along the line the fears began to go beyond the functional purpose of protecting us. They exceeded their limits and became unhealthy. Instead of helping us, they turned on us.

There are three basic fears that can haunt us, and they become destructive. They all have to do with loss:

- loss of life (fear of death)
- loss of place (fear of abandonment)
- loss of face (fear of embarrassment)

These three are the basis for many of the problems we have in social adjustment, social interaction, and social interchange. And they can grow into monsters.

These forms of fear can prevent us from trusting anyone. In an effort to protect ourselves, we simply refuse to show who we really are. We choose to live behind a façade. Living superficially, we get superficial acceptance.

Yet we have a choice: we can allow the fears to cripple us, or we can harness them and make them serve us.

Margaret is so afraid of embarrassment that she can't speak in a group. This has handicapped her at work and kept her from advancing. Hers is fear gone out of control. Craig had the same fear. But instead of crippling him, his fear caused him to take classes to learn some dynamics of public speaking. Now, he not only speaks up in a group, he can lead the group. That's using fear for a positive end: motivation for personal growth.

Joyce is so fearful of being in a car wreck that she can't drive. That's fear being fed for the sake of fear itself. Diane used her fear of driving in Los Angeles traffic to push her to drive defensively, to make sure her car is in good working order, and to drive only when she is alert. She made a servant of her fear.

Charlie's fear of being rejected is so great that he cannot allow himself to take part in social groups. He is serving his fear. Jeff's fear of being rejected causes him to behave in a socially acceptable way, and to keep within the boundaries of both his own and others' personal freedom. He is using the fear to enrich and enhance his life.

Fear that is out of control, fear that is being fed for no purpose other than to nourish itself, fear that has become the master rather than the servant, grows into the monster grandfather dragon. If you do not deal with him, he will eventually kill you.

## Grandmother Dragon Guilt

Grandmother Dragon Guilt is a crafty old dragon. She disguises herself so well, and twists herself into so many shapes, that she can be next to impossible to pin down. Sometimes she even poses as sacred and pretends to be religious. She actually claims to be related to God! One person will claim, *"Guilty? Not me! I never killed anyone!"* while another will cower and cry out *"Guilty!"* for every step he takes in life.

There are two types of guilt: *situational* and *existential*.

## Situational Guilt

Situational guilt is based upon a specific circumstance. It is tied to a particular event at a particular place at a particular time. It is designed to correct our behavior and make us better people. In situational guilt, the healthy goal is forgiveness and reconciliation. It has a beginning and an ending. If it calls us to repentance and causes us to become better people, it is appropriate and healthy. It has a beginning and an end.

While Bonnie was out with a group of girlfriends, someone mentioned Sarah—how cute she was, how slender, well-dressed, and talented. Bonnie was well aware that she was a bit jealous of Sarah. And it just so happened that she had recently overheard a bit of juicy gossip about her. Of course, Bonnie knew she should keep her mouth shut. But out of her own insecurity, she jumped in with, "Speaking of Sarah—did you know she...?"

It worked. Everyone was shocked and disappointed in Sarah.

Immediately, Bonnie wished she had kept quiet. But the damage was done. Bonnie tried to justify her actions to herself—*"After all, it may be true,"* she reasoned. *"Maybe my friends needed to know for their own protection."* But the nagging guilt didn't stop.

Bonnie couldn't take the words back, but she did get honest with herself and recognize that what she did was done out of her own problems. She owned up to it with each of the other girls. Bonnie even went to Sarah and apologized for being jealous and critical of her. Then she laid her guilt to rest.

In this situation, guilt led to growth through forgiveness and reconciliation.

Seven years ago, Henry was involved in an affair. It was

short lived, the woman moved out of town, and his wife never knew. Yet Henry was consumed with guilt. He went to church and prayed for forgiveness. He vowed never to stray again, and he hasn't. And yet today, all these years later, he is still saddled with the guilt.

How does Henry define himself? As an adulterer.

Were Bonnie to come to us, we would say, "Good going. That's over and done with, and you have learned a lesson. Now let's talk about what caused this inside you." Were Henry to come to us, we would say, "So, how long do you need to feel guilty about this? Accept God's forgiveness, forgive yourself, let it go, and move on. Then let's address the real problem—what led you to this behavior.

## Existential Guilt

Unlike situational guilt, *there is no specific reason for existential guilt*. It's not attached to an act, a place, a time, or a thing. Instead of being guilty for what he does, this person is guilty simply for who he is. If he is playing, he should be working. If he is working, he should be playing. If she is at home, she should be at the office. If she is at the office, she should be home. If he did it today, he should have done it yesterday. If he did it yesterday, he should have waited until today. Whatever happens, this person feels he is wrong.

This type of guilt is usually tied to a childhood experience, or a series of experiences. Rarely does it have to do with an objective evaluation of the present.

With this kind of guilt, there is no redemption. There is no forgiveness. It never ends. There is no peace, because it isn't logical or reasonable. We lug it around with us unless and until we make up our minds that: "*I'm responsible for my behavior; I'm not guilty. I'm accountable for my behavior; I'm not to blame.*"

•

There is no place in the life of a healthy person for guilt. If you feel guilty, it is only because of the condemnation you pronounce on yourself.
Responsibility replaces guilt.

•

When a person cannot accept release from guilt, we ask: "What does your guilt do for you that keeps you from giving it up?" Perhaps it:

- makes you feel righteous.
- serves as a substitute internal parent.
- keeps you in line.
- serves as a false control over your life.
- gives you a crutch or excuse.
- _____
  _____
  _____
- _____
  _____
  _____
- _____
  _____
  _____

Now, here is the next question: "What does your guilt do *to* you?" It may:

- keep you depressed.
- prevent you from relaxing.
- not let you enjoy anything.
- make you work harder and longer.
- keep you feeling inferior.
- make you self-conscious and afraid.

- _____
  _____
  _____
- _____
  _____
  _____
- _____
  _____
  _____

Grandmother Guilt and Grandfather Fear are well aware that the hallmarks of the changing person are responsibility and accountability. Therefore, they do all they can to keep you from learning to say,

•

"I'm responsible: I'm not guilty.
I'm accountable; I'm not to blame."

•

## Dragon Food

Your dragons depend on you to keep them well nourished. It's the food you feed them that keeps them alive and well, prospering and reproducing. What is your dragon food of choice? This list of common dragon food will give you an idea of where to start looking.

GRANDFATHER FEAR
  loves:
"What if..."
"I can't..."
"I'll never..."
"What will people think
  if..."

GRANDMOTHER GUILT
  adores:
"I should have..."
"Why did I...?"
"I don't deserve..."
"I have to..."
"It's not my fault..."

"Compared to him, I am..."
"I might make a mistake."
"What if someone finds out?"
"I might fail."
"I might succeed."
"I don't have what it takes."
"I'm not good enough."
"Suppose that..."

"If my parents saw..."
"If people really knew me..."
"I've done it again."
"It's a sin!"
"What would mother think?"
"What would God say?"

If you want guaranteed fear, go to the future. Because you can't do one thing about either of these.

•

You cannot change the past,
and you cannot predict the future.
The only place in time in which you can be free
and have any measure of contentment and
peace is in the present.

•

The present is the only safe place to live.

Most of the time, fear and guilt go together. Guilt produces fear, fear produces guilt. They make a deadly couple. To make matters worse, they are fearfully productive. They don't have babies—they have formidable litters of dragonettes!

## SECOND GENERATION DRAGONS: PAPA DRAGON ANGER AND MAMA DRAGON INADEQUACY

•

From fear springs anger. From guilt
springs inadequacy.

•

140

It happens like this: "If you find out what I am really like, I'm afraid you won't love me. You will leave me or reject me. And that makes me angry with you."

Papa Dragon Anger makes himself known by causing you to say:

- Just look what he did!
- She did this...to me!
- After all I did for her!
- He is not going to get away with that!
- Last week, she...
- Last year, he...

Mama Dragon Inadequacy can make you want to keep people from being close to you. She can show herself by causing you to:

- always try to placate people.
- buy your friendships with favors.
- never say no to anybody for anything.
- keep people indebted to you. (Not "intentionally," of course.)
- please everyone.
- be-all and do-all for everyone.
- keep everyone from getting close enough to know the real you.
- listen to everyone else's problems, but keep your mouth shut about your own.

And we're just beginning to climb the dragon family tree!

## AND MULTITUDES OF DRAGONETTES

Dragonettes by the score rise up to complicate your life. They go by such names as:

- Rage
- Self-hate
- Envy
- Jealousy
- Hatred
- Judgmentalism
- Bitterness
- Criticism
- Childishness
- Blaming
- Negativism

They are a rowdy bunch of troublemakers. And when they enter, they bring along their bratty cousins.

**Dragon Nieces and Dragon Nephews**
Here indeed is a bunch of insolent rascals. Their names are:

- Phobia
- Fetish
- Prejudice
- Bias
- Compulsion
- Obsession
- Panic attacks

Do you see the progression? Grandfather Dragon **Fear** begets Father Dragon **Anger** who fathers Dragonette **Rage** who brings along Nephew Dragon **Prejudice** that leads to untold suffering and persecution. Because when a dragon is not dealt with at one level, it goes on begetting and begetting and begetting. And each generation comes forth stronger and more brazen than the one before.

Oftentimes the dragonettes are a façade behind which older dragons hide to keep from being identified. We might call it *"the dragon in sheep's clothing!"* Kate is a good example:

"My problem," she says, "is that I can't sleep. I go to bed, and something comes into my mind, and I just can't get it out. I toss and turn, wearing out the sheets, thinking about it over and over. I try to tell myself to just forget it for now, that I can't do anything about it at night anyway, but I just can't let go. So that's my problem—sleeplessness."

Kate's problem is not sleeplessness. It's obsession.

You give your life over to the dragons of fear and guilt when you continue to accuse yourself. They live and thrive when, in all of your inner dialogue, there is no voice that says, "God loves me, I love me, I love God, and I am okay."

## CORRALING THE DRAGONS

After you've kept your dragons so long, and have fed them so faithfully, you begin to think of them as sacred. You may even be convinced that you cannot live without them. "Protectors," you may call them, believing that they actually take care of you. You may even begin to think they *are* "the real you."

- "Guilt keeps me from doing things I shouldn't do. If I feel a little bit guilty, it sort of curbs my behavior."

- "My sense of inadequacy keeps me humble. I don't have to accept your compliments. I can keep putting myself down."

- "If I stay fearful of something, it won't actually happen to me."

- "Fear keeps me from making a fool of myself."

- "As long as I am angry about something, I don't have to do anything about it."

If you had a really good reason for not giving up one of your dragons, what would that reason be?

- Do you want to continue a familiar feeling from your childhood?

- Would giving it up mean changing every relationship in your life?

- Is it easier to just keep on feeling guilty?

- Do you know what to do without it?

- Does it keep you in control?

- Does it keep you responsible and on the straight and narrow?

- Does it have a melancholy-type appeal?

- Or are you *supposed* to feel guilty?

Whatever your reason, if you don't want to give your dragons up, keep them a secret. If other people know about your monsters, they likely won't see the value of your feeding and caring for them. Other people might think it is downright ridiculous to hold on to them so tightly.

●

If those dragons continue to live in your basement,
they will suck you dry.

●

This may already be happening. Have you noticed:

- You don't have real belly laughs anymore? Maybe you snicker, perhaps even chuckle, but no one hears a hearty, rollicking laugh from you?

- You only enjoy things in hindsight? Nothing is that exciting while you're doing it. Do you have to look back at it to really enjoy it?

- There's a bit of a lid on everything? Are all your feelings of joy, excitement, anticipation, fun, and laughter somehow diluted?

If your dragons are old enough and strong enough, your clouded emotions will seem normal to you. You've felt guilty, fearful, and inadequate all your life. This is how you learned to view the world.

You do not have to live this way!

You can take charge of change!

You can build a new you!

You are traveling the road you choose to travel. St. George the Dragon Slayer is nothing compared to what you have to be if you're going to conquer your dragons. Knives, swords, and guns are useless against them. You have to grapple with them with your bare heart.

# 11
## BATTLING THE MONSTERS

*"I just decided to shut off the camera,*
*and the movie stopped.*
*It was over."*

Robert Johnson, in his brilliant book entitled *He*, tells the story of an ancient knight named Parsifal.[3]

Parsifal was a knight, brave and noble. He had killed many dragons and captured many enemies. To honor him, a three-day celebration was held in the court of King Arthur. Parsifal had come a long way from the days when he was a poor, nameless boy, born and raised in the cultural backwater on the fringe of the thenknown world. Now here he was, proudly drinking in the praise and adulation of the strongest and bravest of the land.

At the height of the festivities, a hideous damsel burst in and put an instant damper on all the celebration. She appeared on a limping, decrepit old mule. So horrible was she that the royal courts stared at her in shocked silence. Her mission? "...to present the other side of the coin at the festival, a task she accomplishes with genius. She recites all Parsifal's sins and stupidities, the worst being his failure to ask the healing question in the Grail castle. Parsifal is humbled and left silent before the court that only a moment before had been praising him to the sky."

---

[3]*He*, by Robert A. Johnson. Harper & Row Publishers, 1989.
Ibid, page 69.

Like the Hideous Damsel, our dragons crouch in wait for the opportunity to spring out and attack us just when we think we are at our strongest.

## THOSE LURKING DRAGONS

•

If your dragons are lying quietly,
you can be certain they are lying in wait.
Either you will conquer and control them,
or they will conquer and control you.

•

Fred says: "I know a lot about dragons. I kept mine hidden away in the basement of my house in a steel room with walls a foot thick. I had to feed them constantly, and I kept them pushed back and hidden so that their roaring wouldn't frighten the people I was talking to upstairs. I was so ashamed of them that I kept them as far as I could from public view."

When he wasn't feeding his dragons, Fred was throwing them bones to chew on. *"What if such and such happens, then what if so and so happens, then what if...?"* He could worry on and on, day after day.

Finally, with help, Fred found the answer to slaying his dragons: **ADA—Awareness, Decision, Action**.

### Awareness

The first step toward conquering your dragons is to become aware that they exist. As long as we feel guilty, fearful, angry, and inadequate, we know how to:

• act.

- react.
- interact.
- treat others.
- be treated.

But once we are not guilty or afraid, no longer angry or feeling inadequate and worthless, our coping mechanism is gone.

•

Many people would rather live with the familiar guilt than with unfamiliar forgiveness.

•

What a waste of life!

Simply by giving up your denial and becoming willing to acknowledge your dragons, you are taking the first step toward overcoming them.

## Decision

Now that you are aware, control is only a decision away:
*God loves me,*
*I love me,*
*I love God,*
*I am okay.*
*Period.*
*The end.*

This is the best weapon any of us has. And it is a powerful and capable weapon indeed—nothing less than deadly "dragon poison."

Short of making this new decision, everything you do against your dragons will fail. You can never *work* your way out from under them. Every time you feel you might be able to step up to them, they rise up stronger and more fierce. Only by making that new decision can you finally be pronounced, once and for all, *Not Guilty!* When driven deeply into solid rock, that decision is the stake that can finally make you secure enough to stand firm against them. Only there can you live at peace, be happy, plan for the future, and finally get a fresh start on level ground.

**Action**

Is there
- something you need to do?
- restitution you need to make?
- an apology you need to offer?
- forgiveness you need to ask?
- amends that have to be made?

If so, do it.

If this is not possible, then forgive yourself, accept God's forgiveness, and move on. Whether the other person forgives you or not is irrelevant. Your decision must be the same whether those around you do or do not respond appropriately.

Waste no time. The best time of your life lies ahead.

(Too many people who are harboring dragons in their own basements insist on telling everyone else what to do with their dragons. It is very important to *limit your slaying to your own dragons*. Make it a cardinal rule to keep your hands off other people's monsters.)

## FIVE CHARACTERISTICS OF A HIGHLY SUCCESSFUL DRAGON SLAYER

There are five characteristics that identify people who are successfully slaying their dragons.

## Characteristic #1: They Are Aware of Their Feelings

Successful dragon slayers know and understand their own emotions. They can name their feelings. Unless and until you begin to claim your own internal emotional state, you cannot rid yourself of those troublesome beasts.

If you are angry and don't know it, you are going to injure yourself or someone else.

If you're depressed and don't claim it, you're going to damage yourself or someone else.

If you're sad and don't recognize it, you're going to hurt yourself or someone else.

•

The first and primary characteristic of mentally healthy people is that they know what is going on inside themselves.

•

You are a whole being made up of many parts. Three of them are:

**Physical** — You are a physical being. Whether you are asleep or awake, your body continues to work.

**Mental** — Your brain works all the time, whether you are conscious or unconscious, as long as you are alive.

**Emotional** — You have feelings all the time. They never stop, either.

You concentrate a great deal on your physical well being. You eat, you sleep, you exercise, you bathe, you comb your hair, and you groom your body. You also spend time and energy on your mental self. You challenge it. You learn new things. But what about your emotional self? If you are like most people, it is that part of you that gets short-changed. Consider this: It has been said that the human eye can decipher 124 million hues of color. Yet most people have five or six, maybe seven, words to describe their emotions. So much color possibility, so little emotional acknowledgment!

Without a way to express your feelings, it will be difficult for you to conquer your dragons and build healthy intimate relationships. Until you can tell both yourself and another person what you feel, there is going to be a dimension of yourself that neither of you will ever know.

So let's work on building an emotional vocabulary. Write down 30 or more words for emotions. (We started the list for you.)

happy

depressed

mad

angry

excited

joyful

frustrated

embarrassed

ecstatic

peaceful

Make a copy of this list and carry it with you in your pocket or your purse. Pull it out when you're standing in line at the grocery store or at the ATM window, when you're waiting on a traffic light, when you take a break to stretch your legs at the office. Go down your list and ask yourself, "What am I feeling right now?" In time you will find that you are becoming skilled at expressing exactly what's happening to you emotionally.

Eventually you will have a rich emotional vocabulary in your head from which you can draw at any time and under any circumstance.

## Characteristic #2: They Claim Their Feelings

When someone else can tell you more about your feelings than you are willing to admit, you need to catch up with the conversation. When someone looks at you and says, *"I know you're angry,"* and you yell back, *"I AM NOT ANGRY!"* you need to stop, step back, and pull it together again.

•

Feelings are neither good nor bad.
They are neither right nor wrong. It's what you do
with feelings that determines whether they have a
good or bad, right or wrong, effect.

•

It is a genuine mark of maturity to be able to say, "Right now I'm feeling angry (insecure, threatened, sad, anxious, happy, excited, elated)." Those feelings are characteristics of who you are. And who you are comes out best in the expressions of your emotions.

Don't be frightened by your feelings. They are okay. You feel one thing right now, but you're going to feel something else a little bit later. Give yourself permission to say, *"I am so happy right now!"* And it's just as okay to say, *"I feel dreadful!"*

Once you are that aware of your emotions, if someone should ask, "What are you feeling?" you will be able to give an immediate answer. Then again, you may choose *not* to answer. That's fine. The important thing is that you will be aware of your feelings. Because what we're not aware of controls us. Either we express our behavior, or we act it out.

## Characteristic #3: They Are Responsible for Their Feelings

*"It's not my fault. I just lost my temper!"*
Passing responsibility seems to be the current American way. But when you take responsibility for your own feelings and behavior, you can no longer fall back on those same old excuses. You'll find your excuse list for harmful words or actions pared way down.

•

When you accept responsibility for your own feelings, you are well on the road to emotional health and happiness.

•

## Characteristic #4: They Are Sensitive to the Feelings of Others

Once you accept the responsibility for your own feelings, an amazing thing happens: you become sensitive and responsive to the feelings and needs of other people. Suddenly there is an entirely new color and dimension to your personality.

- You relate to others in a different way.
- You behave differently in social situations.
- You are more aware of, and accepting of, differences in people.
- You develop a new tolerance toward others.

•

As a changing person, your acute sensitivity makes
you safe to be with.

•

It makes you desirable as a companion and friend. It also gives you a sense of belonging.

## Characteristic #5: They Are in Charge

When you are in charge of yourself and your relationships, you have achieved a wonderful dimension of freedom and privilege. You are safe. You don't need to attach to someone else, or to manipulate in a relationship. You can affirm and compliment other people.

You can now experience a level of life qualitatively higher than ever before. Life is more than the search for food, clothing, and shelter. It is larger than "Me and my wife, son John and his wife, us four and no more." It is bigger than your race and religion. It is broader than your heritage. It is deeper than your philosophy. It is wider than your knowledge and understanding.

•

People in charge make society as a whole
authentic and life bearable.

•

They send out messages of safety, meaning, and purpose to everyone around them. These are the true knights and ladies of our times. They are the ones who have conquered their dragons. The quality and peace they bring into relationships empower others and allow themselves to be stronger and more successful in their own right.

## DRAGON HABITS

When we examine them closely, we see that Grandfather and Grandmother Dragon are nothing more than second-hand, shopworn old habits. And like all habits, they can be overcome.

When the old habits are replaced by new ones, you will find that you have an exciting person to take around with you, to work with and play with, day in and day out. This someone is loved and secure and comfortable to be with.

•

The new person is—you!

•

With the help of a psychiatrist, Fred got the courage to drive his dragons out of his basement, one by one. They all fizzled in the sunlight and died. Afterward, his psychiatrist asked, "What are you going to do with that room that used to be the dragon's lair?"

"I don't know," Fred answered.

"Well," the doctor suggested, "why don't you make it into a chapel and use it as a place of worship?"

Today, in place of the nasty dragon den, our friend has a throne room, a beautiful place of wonder, worship, and celebration.

What will you make out of your old dragon lair?

# 12
# TAKE CONTROL OF YOUR LIFE!

*"Honey, I decided years ago not to love anything
that doesn't love me back."*

We have worked with all kinds of people who want to
change their lives—people of all ages, all nationalities and
races, all walks of life. The youngest was a boy we'll call
Matthew and the oldest was a woman we'll call Edith.

Matthew was seven years old when he called us on the
telephone and said, "You talked to my mother and daddy.
Mama said I could have anything I wanted for my birthday and I want to come there and see you. Can I come?"

We asked Matthew why he wanted to come to Texas
and see us.

"Because my mother and daddy are really, really happy
now, and I want you to do to me what you did to them."

Edith was 84 when she came to see us. Besides her
grandchildren, she was the only one in her family still living. Her parents, siblings, husband, and son had all died,
and she came to us because of her depression. She came
ready to change, and she did.

"I can tell by looking at you young girls that I've let my
wardrobe go far too long," she said to the 40- and 50-
years-olds in our office. "I've got to get myself spiffed up.
All I wear is beige clothes! I've got to get rid of this stuff
and get some color into my life."

•

## You are not too young to change, and you are not too old.

•

## YOU AT 90

Picture self on your 90th birthday. You are in a nursing home. Your family and the couple of friends who are still alive are there with the other residents. They sing an off-key version of "Happy Birthday to You," but it doesn't matter that it's not that melodic. You can't hear much anymore anyway. There is a big cake, chocolate with white frosting, topped with so many lighted candles you're afraid it will set off the fire alarm.

No one stays long. They worry about "tiring" you out. So before you know it, you are back in your room.

What are you going to wish you had done in your life? People give all kinds of answers to this question. They say:

- I wish I'd learned to play the piano.
- I wish I'd earned a college degree.
- I wish I'd seen where my dad was raised in Alaska.
- I wish I had traveled around the country.
- I wish I had spent time with my grandchildren.
- I wish I had taken the vacations from work I was entitled to.
- I wish I had gotten married again.
- I wish I'd had a close friend.
- I wish I had been more soft-spoken and less irritable.
- I wish I had written more notes of appreciation.
- I wish I hadn't been afraid to sing "The Star-Spangled Banner."
- I wish I had used the good china and silver every day.

- I wish I'd seen a space shuttle lift off.
- I wish I'd run a marathon.
- I wish I had organized and labeled the photographs so that I could enjoy them in my old age.
- I wish I had told my family how much I loved them.

Make a list of the things you want to do in your own life. Put down small things and big ones, things you could have done within yourself and things you could have done around you. List personal things just for you, and things to do for others.

This is not a one-time-only list. As you think of new possibilities, add them. You will begin to notice an amazing thing—you will actually be accomplishing many of the things on your list.

Your list is a picture of what you want the rest of your life to look like. You may not do everything, but so what? It doesn't cost anything to dream. And it just might be that even the most impossible will happen.

You may find yourself protesting: *"It sounds great, but I don't feel like I can do any of those things."*

Don't allow your feelings to defeat you! Step up and change them.

**Step #1: Ask Yourself, *"What Am I Feeling?"***

Is your feeling creating a problem for you? If not, if you are completely content and happy with where you are and where you are going, leave well enough alone.

**Step #2: Ask Yourself, *"Is This Feeling Real or Fantasy?"***

We term a feeling *real* if it's tied to a specific place,

event, or time. We term a feeling *fantasy* if it is just free-floating. ("I don't know, nothing really happened. I just woke up feeling that way.")

## Step #3: Determine, *"If the Feeling is a Fantasy, I Will Drop It."*

Recognize the fantasy for what it is. It came from nowhere, and it's going nowhere. It's probably one of those familiar bad-habit feelings. So change your behavior and start acting like you don't feel that way, and eventually you won't.

## Step #4: Determine, *"If the Feeling Is Real, I'll Deal with It."*

Ask yourself, *"What can I do about this feeling that is blocking my way? Can I change my behavior? Can I go back and redo something? Can I ask for an apology? Can I get help with it?"* If yes, do it, then drop the feeling. If no, just drop the feeling!

If these four steps don't work for you, ask yourself, *"Am I holding onto this 'I can't' feeling because it has become a familiar feeling to me? Am I too afraid to reach beyond it? Am I still holding on to feelings from my past?"*
Let go! Live in the present.

•

Here and now, right today, you are responsible for yourself spiritually, physically, and emotionally.

•

**Spiritually**          *Decide to believe.*

God loves me,

I love me,
I love God.

**Physically**        *Decide to take care of your body.*

This means you will provide
food, clothing, safety, shelter,
and exercise for yourself.

**Emotionally**        *Decide to take charge of your
own emotions.*

No one can make you feel.
Your feelings are yours. Claim
them, express them, and move
on.

## SET APPROPRIATE GOALS

Some of the items on your list are readily achievable
(organize my photos, write more notes of appreciation).
Those are things you can start on immediately.

Others, however, seem hopelessly out of reach (climb
Mt. Everest, write a novel). That doesn't mean you have to
give up on those more lofty goals. It just means you need
to set some shortterm goals that will help you reach them.
Let's use writing a novel as an example:

LONG TERM GOAL:        Write a novel.

SHORT TERM GOALS:        Take an adult education
writing course.
Keep a journal.
Read about the craft of writing.

Read novels. Write short
vignettes.
Write short stories.
Plan out my novel.

That novel won't happen today or tomorrow—not even this year, and probably not next year. But, if you work through the progression of bite-sized short-term goals, that novel will very likely be written.

Look over your list at the things you want to accomplish. Which of those things can you do at any time, with the resources you have? Put a ✓. Now look at the ones you couldn't check.

Put a ✓ beside them, labeling them as *long-term goals*. These are the ones for which you may first need short-term goals. Ask yourself:

- What do I need to have or do in order to achieve this goal?
- What are the steps I need to take?
- What is the first step?
- When will I take this step?

Now and then someone insists he just cannot think of any goals: *"I have enough trouble keeping up with my day-to-day life without setting goals for the future."*

If that's the case, forget about long-term goals for now. Think instead of short-term goals. What would give you a great sense of relief or pleasure if you did it within the next month?

*"I've been wanting to get rid of all that stuff stacked up in the garage."*

That's a good goal. But it would take you an entire day, and you probably don't have an entire day. Short-*short* term goals would allow you to achieve it in small chunks. For instance, each of these could be a short-short term goal:

- Separate the boxes of stuff from the piles of stuff.
- Put like things together (car maintenance materials, Christmas decorations, outgrown clothing, and so forth).
- Throw away as much trash as possible.
- Hold a garage sale.

The point is to get off that dead-center, no-action spot. Allow yourself the feeling of accomplishment.

Be specific about your approach:
- When are you going to start?
- What date?
- What time that day?
- What will you eliminate in order to have the time for the task?

## BE HONEST AND REALISTIC

In the excitement of making the list, it's easy to get carried away and make it into a "dream list." If you have a disability, don't put down a goal that would require a miraculous healing. If your parents are no longer living, don't list learning to communicate with them. If the items on your list are unachievable, you will quickly become discouraged and give up the whole thing.

On the other hand, don't be too quick to discard something as "impossible." More people make this mistake than the former one. People say, *"If only I weren't so old, I might...,"* or *"If I were a man instead of a woman, I would...,"* or *"If I just had talent, I could...."*

- Is your age really a factor? (People in their 70s and 80s get college degrees.)

- Is sex really a barrier? (There are few areas today that are not available to both sexes.)

- Do you really need to have talent? (Many people get a great deal of enjoyment out of playing the piano or painting with water colors simply for their own pleasure.)

As we were winding up our visit at the Menninger Clinic in Topeka, Kansas, we sat in with Dr. Karl Menninger as he discussed cases with various professionals. Dr. Menninger, 90-years-old, was still carrying a patient load, as well as keeping up correspondence with over a hundred prisoners. After the meeting, we suggested doing something together with him and his wife. "Actually, I have to leave now," he told us. "It's a little late, and my teacher is going to be waiting for me.

*Teacher?*

"I'm learning Greek," he explained.

At the age of 90, Dr. Menninger had started studying Greek. Why? "Because it is a fascinating language," he told us. He was learning simply for the sake of learning.

## GET GOING!

It's time to set plans in motion that will help you achieve your goals.

Be sure your goals are stated in concrete terms. You say you are going to start an exercise program? What is that program going to be? State it specifically: *I will walk for 30 minutes, from 5:30-6:00, on Mondays, Wednesdays, and Fridays.* You say you are going to take some time to kick back and have fun? When exactly? State: *I'm going to start taking every third Thursday off, and I'm going to use that time to ...."*

You *can* accomplish your goals. Once you make the decision and formulate a plan, once you make yourself aware of it and claim it, your brain will get busy making it happen.

Put your brain on alert, and set it to listen to what it needs to do in order to accomplish what you want.

Your conscious effort is vitally important.

•

Spend your time and energy making plans
to yourself. Stay in charge of those plans.

•

Start telling yourself:

- I am happy!
- I am fulfilled!
- I do enjoy my life!
- I have an increasing number of friends!
- I have personal security!
- I have personal satisfaction!
- I will enjoy life more in the days, weeks, months, and years ahead than I have in any other time of my life!

## LIVE IN THE PRESENT

In the present, you can handle almost anything. Living well today ensures a good future and good memories of the past. This internal permission comes along with the new decision you made about your acceptance by God and by yourself. It states that you will:

- achieve whatever level you choose to achieve.
- experience life at whatever level you want to experience it.
- have as much happiness as you want.
- experience friendship to the ultimate.

You are entitled to all these things. You have conquered your dragons. Like Parsifal, you have a perfect right to stride right into King Arthur's banquet hall and receive all the acclaim and praise and reward you earned for your success in the dragon wars. Never mind the accusations of the Hideous Damsel. Your guilt and fear have been defeated.

If you stay in the present, there are few things you can't handle. It's when you get depressed over what happened back then, and anxious about what will happen tomorrow, that your life starts feeling overwhelmed and unmanageable.

On one of our trips to the Menninger Clinic, Dr. Menninger took Marion Sue Jones and John DeFoore to visit an area called the Children's Villages just outside of Topeka, a venture designed, promoted, and accomplished by Dr. Karl Menninger and his wife, Jean. Young people of various ages who were unable to live in their own homes lived there in residence homes. They were schooled there, had recreation facilities, and were provided everything else they needed. We were eager to tour it to see what it looked like and how it was orchestrated.

The person in charge showed us through the facility. We busily collected statistics on such things as how many kids lived there, how the organization was managed, how the school was run and by whom, what the length of stay was, and so forth. In the middle of our note-taking, we turned around and were surprised to see that Dr. Menninger was no longer with us.

*"We've come all the way out here to see this organization*

*he designed and executed,"* we thought, *"and now he's gone. Where is he?"*

We could hear all the children laughing and playing in the next room. We walked through the door, and there was Dr. Menninger sitting at a table playing dominoes with the kids. He was happy to leave the records of what was and the planning for what was to come to others. Dr. Menninger, one of the greatest men of the century, was busy living in the present with the children!

## CHOOSE TO BE HAPPY

How happy do you choose to be? How rich and full a life will you live? Are you the *agent* of change in your life? Are you the one in control?

Here is your challenge:

•

Deal with the past.
Decide to live in the present.
Determine to take charge of your life and confidently steer it toward your goal.

•

Now step forward in life—*happily!*

# As Happy As You Want To Be!

# About the Authors

In business together since 1974, Marion Sue Jones and John DeFoore own Consultant Services in Boerne, Texas. Marion Sue and John provide counseling and consulting services to individuals, couples, families, and businesses with a therapeutic model they designed years ago. They have worked as therapists in over a dozen countries across the globe, as well as many states in the United States. They have facilitated weekend workshops attended by more than 100 families. Their work as consultants has included senior executives from businesses both in the US and the Far East. They regularly see people in their offices to deal with various issues. Some of the many issues that clients bring to Marion Sue and John include family conflict, coping with loss, navigating major life changes, dealing with anger, depression, setting goals to achieve life satisfaction, and business succession planning. Today, the clinical team of professionals at Consultant Services includes John's son Marney Wayne DeFoore.

By teaching principles that enable people to let go of their past and to manage their personal lives more effectively, the authors have helped hundreds of individuals learn how to improve their personal relationships, achieve greater self-esteem, enjoy a more balanced lifestyle, and attain the power to accept responsibility for personal well-being and happiness.

**For more information, please contact:**
Consultant Services
229 N. Main Street
Boerne, TX 78006
Phone: 830/249-3660
Fax: 830/249-3810
Website: www.consultantservices.org

# Notes

# Notes

# Notes

# Notes

# Notes

# Notes

# Notes

# Notes

# Notes

# Notes